THE SRA/WSRA GUIDE TO BETTER SQUASH

Published in the same series by Pan Books

The PGA European Tour Guide to Better Golf
The LTA Guide to Better Tennis
The British Ski Federation Guide to Better Skiing

Forthcoming

The Amateur Athletic Association Guide to Better Athletics
The Amateur Swimming Association Guide to Better Swimming

THE SRA/WSRA GUIDE TO BETTER SQUASH

CLAIRE CHAPMAN

BOB LINCOLN

JANE POYNDER

PAUL WRIGHT

Photographs by Tommy Hindley and Stephen Line

Pan Books London and Sydney

Contents

InterCity

(Opposite) Rustim Bativala's play has astonished as well as defeated Graeme White in the 1985 InterCity Challenge final

Foreword

Philip Kenyon, the 1986 British Champion, shows the guts and determination he advocates for the budding world class player

Squash is one of the hardest individual sports played today. It demands a great deal of fitness, self motivation, discipline and determination in order to play at a high level. One gratifying thing about squash is that it can be enjoyed by all, and you can set yourself individual targets, from beating a business colleague or challenging club merit orders, to beating your boyfriend or girlfriend. All of this can give satisfying rewards if you win, as you are on your own in a squash court and no one else can help you.

I played tennis to a high standard for a few years, taught by my parents, and it was quite by chance that I started playing squash. I started at the age of eleven, after being inquisitive about a strange-looking racket brought home by my father. I then proceeded to learn more about this game called squash! Three months later I was trying to master the art of the game. I took to it very rapidly: my ball sense was never a problem. After two years of being coached by my father, I was asked if I wanted to be coached professionally. There was an opportunity to be coached by Clive Francis, who at that time was the British professional champion. I accepted,

Davies&Tate
Replacement Window Systems

as I was beginning to get hooked, as many people do.

Within eighteen months I was Lancashire and Cheshire Junior Champion; I dropped all other sports and squash was my spare-time occupation. Fortunately, I have always been self-motivated and started training for the sport, running five miles each day, skipping at a rate of 4000 skips each day, and 100 sit-ups per day. The hard work was all worthwhile when I became three times British Junior Champion and World Junior Champion, and held a string of other titles.

I was still living at home at nineteen years of age until I took and passed all the important exams – GCEs, a diploma in food technology, as well as certificates in business management and organization, book-keeping and accountancy. Now a lot more people are going full-time into squash at the age of fifteen, but are getting lost along the way to becoming a professional. This is due to a lack of discipline and self-commitment and thinking that it will all come too easily. I can assure anyone who is thinking of becoming a world class player that you need a lot of guts and determination, and if you enjoy living out of a suitcase for months on end it will help.

I have now been playing professional squash for seven years and have fortunately been relatively free of injury. This has a lot to do with body conditioning and exercises. I stretch each time before playing and strengthen my muscles by using weights. This continuous programme has enabled me to win two British Under 23 titles, four British Closed titles, two European titles as well as fifty major tournaments, too many to mention.

In squash you need lots of support and guidance whether it be from a coach, a friend, a mentor or your wife. Do not be afraid to criticise yourself frequently and make changes for the better; you will never be perfect. I have been fortunate to have what I consider the best of both worlds: my wife Charmaine travels with me most of the time and acts as my mentor, friend, wife, companion and supporter; a hard task for anyone, but it works well for us.

For everyone who wishes to play squash may I wish you every success in the sport. What you put into your practice and training will be rewarded in your game. Good squash!

Philip Kenyon and Qamar Zaman compete for the dominant position on the 'T'

LUCY SOUTTER

Foreword

1986 British Champion Lucy Soutter, fully stretched but still perfectly balanced to play the shot

Sport, fitness and the game of squash in particular are a way of life for me. I have been playing for ten years already, since I was eight years old. In the beginning I played squash throughout the winter, moving to tennis in the summer, continuing in this way until I was fourteen, when I finally decided to make a choice. In retrospect, the decision was relatively easy, as I was far better at squash and had just won the British Under Sixteens Open Title for the first time at the age of thirteen. Leaving school in the summer of 1983 with six O levels, I went on to win the Under Sixteens title twice more, and also the Under Nineteens Open Championship twice. These titles helped to give me the confidence to branch further afield, and to try to break into the senior rankings.

I now find myself not only the World Junior Champion but British Women's number one and World number three, having quite quickly climbed through the ranks. This is due to a variety of reasons. Firstly, I have had fantastic home support and encouragement – my family are all keen players, especially my father, who has been a major influence on my squash success. I have never been forced to play. However, the support and help have

always been there. In recent times my coach Ian McKenzie has taught me a great deal about physical, mental and tactical approaches to the game. It is important to have a coach like Ian, to give advice and add new dimensions to your game. Everyone needs a little help now and then! Nevertheless, at the end of the day there is no substitute for hard work and effort, dedication and motivation being the key words. While still at school I found people very ready to make fun of me when I was going off to practise or if I refused an invitation to a disco. However, it's amazing how things change – now they might even come to watch!

They say that school days are the best days of your life; but I can't agree as my life at present is far more satisfying and enjoyable. The travelling involved in squash, together with the experience of meeting so many different people from such an early age, has helped me to grow up with a balanced attitude towards life in general, and has given me considerable self-confidence. I don't feel at all that I have missed out on any aspect of life. I would advise anyone thinking of taking up full-time squash to keep your options open for the first few years, enjoying a variety of activities; but after serious contemplation to knuckle down and work hard, as that's where the success comes from. And above all, enjoy it!

(Opposite) Lucy Soutter packs a powerful drive in a small frame. Note the light-coloured ball used on the see-through perspex court

(Below) Lucy Soutter is forced on the defensive by the hard hitting Martine le Moignan

JANE POYNDER

Part One: Getting started

Squash rackets came into being as a hybrid of rackets, a game traditionally played at English public schools. Rackets is played with a hard ball, similar to a small cricket ball, but boys waiting to play were allowed to practise outside the rackets court with a soft rubber ball, no doubt to avoid breaking windows.

Squash grew in popularity but for a long time retained its public school connections. Many of the first courts in England were built at public schools, in large country houses and in the services. It was introduced as well to other countries where there was a strong colonial and military influence, such as India, Pakistan and Egypt.

The first official men's championships was held in 1923. The women had their first event in 1922. Early champions in the game came from England, but Egypt and Pakistan soon dominated the championship roll. It was not until 1966 that this overseas dominance was brought to a halt by an Irishman from Cornwall called Jonah Barrington! – pictured opposite.

Barrington's emergence has had a lasting influence on squash in Britain. The squash boom of the middle 60s and 70s produced squash courts in abundance all over the country, in private members clubs, commercial clubs and in public sports centres. Squash has now taken its place as one of the largest participation sports, and whilst the 'boom' of the 70s has been replaced by the 'consolidation' of the 80s there are now well over three million squash players in Britain. At least one third of these are women.

Prior to 1928 squash in England was controlled by the Tennis and Rackets Association. In 1928 it was decided to form the Squash Rackets Association solely to look after squash. A Ladies Committee was appointed to look after the needs of women in the game and in 1934 the Women's Squash Rackets Association was formed. Since then English squash has been looked after by these two bodies who are autonomous in overall control but who work very closely together in all areas of the game.

Nearly all the major competitive events are now run jointly for both men and women. 1986 saw the staging of the first National Championships, formerly the British Closed Event. Both this and the British Open Championships were played on an all-perspex court, which together with the development of a 'television' ball is quickly turning squash into a spectator sport as well as a major participant sport.

STARTING TO PLAY

Squash has a very wide competitive structure and this is perhaps one of the reasons for its great popularity. As it is not a difficult game technically, the beginner can often enjoy a degree of competition right from the start.

Most towns and sometimes even villages now have a squash club, either attached to an existing sporting facility such as a municipal sports centre or as part of a tennis, rugby or hockey club. Many clubs provide introductory coaching sessions for beginners to the game. Competition is readily available through club 'social' evenings, club leagues and ultimately club matches.

There is a strong emphasis on junior development and competition in squash and there is now almost as much international and national junior competition as senior.

If you are unsure how to get started, contact your national Squash Rackets Association who should be able to put you in touch with a club or a coach in your area (see page 142).

As with most sports, the younger you are when you begin playing squash the easier it is to develop a sound technique which should help you progress up the competitive ladder. However, it is a game which can be taken up at all ages providing you prepare for it sensibly. Squash is a hard, vigorous game and you do need to be FIT for it!

You can learn a lot from watching good players in action. Try to attend some of the major championships. Some events are televised but it is obviously more exciting to attend in person.

Jahangir Khan – the dominant player of the 1980s – took up the game at a very early age

EQUIPMENT

Having decided where you are going to play squash you must have the necessary equipment.

Sports equipment is something of a boom industry so it is worth shopping around before making your purchase. Many sports shops will give a discount to members of clubs within a certain area. Clubs often have a professional coach who runs his own shop where again better local rates may be offered.

Rackets

Rackets can be made of wood, carbon fibre graphite, ceramics and fibreglass. Racket technology is developing all the time and at present graphite rackets have become more popular than the more conventional wooden ones. When selecting a racket, swing it around in your hand and make certain that it feels right for you. It should not feel heavy and unwieldy, but rather like a wand with which you will be able to generate racket head speed with good timing and little physical effort. Choose between a conventional or slightly larger size racket head. The larger head will give you a bigger hitting area, but make sure that it feels in proportion to the balance of the racket.

Grip size can vary as can the type of grip on the racket handle. Make certain that the size of handle is suitable for you. Towel handles are popular but need to be changed regularly to keep their absorbancy. Rubberized tape and reverse calf grips will help you maintain a good hold on the racket in even the hottest courts. Leather grips are also popular. Synthetic leather grips are not recommended as they tend to become extremely slippery when the hand gets hot.

Top quality rackets are usually strung with natural gut but there are many synthetic guts which are very similar in effect and may suit you just as well.

One of the many graphite rackets now used by the top players

Clothing

For competitive play, predominantly white clothing or matching pastel shades are permitted. Some squash centres may permit more extreme coloured clothing but remember it is sometimes more difficult to sight the ball if your opponent is wearing dark clothing. Clothing should be comfortable and absorbant.

It is essential to have shoes that have a non marking, preferably white sole. Black or dark rubber soles are never permitted as they mark the floor of the court.

When selecting squash shoes make sure that the sole has plenty of grip and that the shoe is very flexible. Also check the height of the heel tab. A high stiff heel tab can cause discomfort and can ultimately damage the tendon through constant chafing.

If your movement is hindered by sore feet and blisters caused by rubbing shoes then your game will suffer. Take care of your 'tires' and wear socks which absorb perspiration. Never wear thin nylon, non-absorbant socks!

White soles and a good grip are essential in squash shoes

SAFETY

Off court preparation

Squash is a hard strenuous game so it is advisable to do some physical preparation before you go on the court. This simple check list should help you perform better.

1 If you are a newcomer to the game and are somewhat advanced in years ensure that you are reasonably physically fit before you play. A check up with your doctor is sometimes advisable and many squash clubs can now give you a test to check your pulse rate.

2 Always try to do some physical warming up before you play. This should include a pulse warmer to get you ready for action and some stretching exercises to warm up your muscles and thus help to prevent injury.

3 Never play squash if you have a fever!

On court

As the game is played in close proximity to the opponent it is essential that you swing your racket safely and avoid striking the ball if you are in a position where it is likely to hit your opponent.

It is worthwhile studying the rules of the game so that you understand your rights as a player. In some instances obstruction will mean the award of a stroke to the player who has been prevented from playing a shot. However, in the early stages of your squash the most important thing to remember is not to hit the ball if you might hit your opponent!

No racket is guaranteed against breakage and even Martine le Moignan, one of England's leading players, couldn't win with this one

FUNDAMENTALS OF SQUASH

You can obtain a copy of the complete rules of squash from your national Squash Rackets Association (see page 142), but if you are just starting to play, the following summary will give you a basic understanding of how the game works.

SCORING

Squash is normally played over the best of 5 games. Women play the same as men.

Each game is played to 9 points and points are scored only by the server. If you win the rally as the receiver you then win the right to serve.

In American scoring, however, points are scored by the receiver as well as the server.

EIGHT ALL

Should a game reach 8–8 the *receiver* can elect to play 'set two' which means that the game is played to ten points, or 'no set' which means that the game is played to nine points. The game never goes beyond ten points.

NEW GAME

The player who wins the previous game always serves first in the next game.

SERVICE BOX

The server may choose whether to serve from the left or right box but assuming he wins the rally the next service must be taken from the opposite box.

THE SPIN

The players spin a racket to see who will serve first. The winner of the spin serves first.

REST

Much as you might like a pause between rallies the game should be played continuously and in fact if you do waste time your opponent could be awarded a stroke, a game, or even the match. You are allowed one minute's rest between games and two minutes' rest between the fourth and fifth game when you may need it!

THE SERVICE

The server must stand with at least one foot in the service box and must have this contact with the box until the ball has been struck. If he fails to do this it is a footfault.

The ball must be struck above the cut line and must land in the opponent's back quarter of the court. If it fails to reach this area but remains within the boundary of the court then it is a fault and if the receiver makes no attempt to hit it a second service will be taken. The receiver can take a single fault service on the first service, in which case the rally must then continue.

If a fault is struck on the second service then the receiver automatically wins the rally whether he attempts to hit the ball or not.

If the ball is missed completely by the server, or hits either the boundary line or above, or the tin, then the server immediately loses the rally.

THE PLAY

The ball remains in play until it is struck either on or above the boundary line, or hits the tin. If the opponent fails to reach the ball before it has bounced twice the rally is over.

Marker and Referee in a good position to control this match between Qamar Zaman and Magdi Saad

THE OFFICIALS
If you play in a match both a marker and a referee should officiate. If there is only one official he undertakes all duties.

Duties of the marker

Introduces the match.
Controls the spectators.
Calls the score.
Calls fault or foot fault as appropriate.
Calls the ball out, not up or down as appropriate.
OUT=Ball on or above the boundary line
NOT UP=Ball reached after it has bounced twice.
DOWN=Ball hit into the tin.
Repeats the decisions made by the referee, namely no let, let when the rally is replayed, or award a stroke.

Duties of the referee

Ensures fair play and sees that neither player is infringing the rules whether through obstruction, time wasting or argument.

Checks the marker, so also records the score.

Answers appeals from the players on marker's call or lack of call.

Answers appeals from the players in cases of obstruction.

Keeps the time. Supervises 5 minute knock up, rest between games.

As the referee has to make a judgement as to whether a player has been obstructed it is an important and essential role in competitive squash. It is therefore advisable to study this aspect of the game. Courses are run for refereeing and marking and information on this aspect of the game can be obtained from the Squash Referee's Society.

The court

Squash is played in a rectangular court 32 feet (9.75m) long and 21 feet (6.40m) wide.

The walls are made of a non sweating plaster and the floor of hard wood, ideally non varnished, i.e. unsealed.

Pay particular attention to the floor of the court as the speed of movement required in the game necessitates a sound foot hold. Floors which are 'over sealed' will appear shiny and will be slippery.

While the dimensions of a court are strictly laid down, the height may vary and may affect your tactical play. Notice how high the court is and how the lights are positioned on the ceiling. If your ball passes through the chains suspending the lights then it is out.

The temperature of a court can have a very strong influence on the type of game a player may play. Court temperatures can vary tremendously and you should take account of this when planning your tactics.

Balls

Different types of ball are available to help you cope with varying court temperatures and standarads of play. A squash ball needs to be warm, lively and bouncy to

BALL CHART

double yellow dot	very slow	championship play high altitude play	advanced players
yellow dot	slow	most competitive play in warm courts	competition players of all levels
white dot	medium	competitive play in very cold conditions	good players in cold conditions juniors beginners in warm courts
red dot	fast	cold courts	beginners good players wishing to simulate hot court conditions
blue dot	very fast	very cold courts	complete beginners

produce a good game. If the ball feels heavy and dead when you strike it then you are using one which is not suitable for the court conditions and your standard of play. Study the chart and select a ball which is appropriate to your needs and you will have a more enjoyable game.

Balls may be made of either green, blue or black rubber. Many clubs advocate the use of the green ball as it helps to keep squash court walls cleaner. The *black* ball is used for all major competitions. In major events a special white 'television' ball has been introduced to improve the sighting of the ball on the T.V. monitor.

COURT CHART

hot/warm courts	ball bounces higher/ faster	rallies longer	players need to be fitter and more patient; ball more difficult to hit as a winner
cold courts	ball bounces slower and lower	shorter rallies, easier to play winners	players need to be quicker to retrieve short low shots

SIMPLE TACTICS

As you are playing in a rectangular court the tactically advantageous position to be in is in the middle, namely the 'T'. Try always to return to it between shots.

Play your shots as close to the side walls as you are able and direct them towards one of the four corners of the court, ideally the one furthest away from the opponent.

Watch the ball constantly, as you will then know where your opponent is and what shot he is about to play. This is especially important when the ball and the opponent are behind you. As well as giving you a tactical advantage it should help to prevent you obstructing your opponent's shot towards the front wall. Remember you have to give him freedom to play the shot of his choice to any part of the front wall, so you must keep out of the line of this shot. If you are unable to do so it is likely that the stroke will be awarded to him. As you can only score points when you are the server it is tactically advisable to play more cautiously when you are receiver. Attack when you are winning and defend aggressively when you are losing.

The opponent

Study your opponent and try to adapt your game to make it as difficult as possible for him.

Observe the following:

1 Is he right or left handed?

2 Fast or slow about the court?

3 Which strokes in his game appear effective and which may break down under prolonged pressure?

4 Does he seem fit?

5 Where does he play his winning shots?

(Opposite) Barbara Diggens watching the action behind her as the Australian Rhonda Thorne plays one of her excellent boasts

(Right) Sue Cogswell, a former British Champion and a masterly stroke player, directs the ball to one of the front corners against Vicky Cardwell of Australia

CLAIRE CHAPMAN

Part Two: Basic technique

Sound technique makes it easy to play consistent, accurate shots and once learnt is never forgotten; so time spent on this in the early stages is worthwhile.

The photographs and descriptions are all of a right-handed player so left-handed players will have to reverse all the left/rights to understand the technique.

For the sake of brevity, 'He' has been used throughout the book to refer to an opponent or partner.

Some terms used in the descriptions may not be familiar to beginners and these are defined below.

Sound technique – one of the hallmarks of world champions Jahangir Khan and New Zealand's Susan Devoy

GLOSSARY OF TERMS

'T'
The 'T' is literally the junction between the half-court line and the short line on the floor of the court. As used in the book, it describes the commanding position to which you should always try to return, which is about two feet (⅔ metre) behind the junction.

GOOD LENGTH
A shot which bounces for the second time very close to the back wall.

COCKED WRIST
The position, shown in the photograph, from which all the strokes are started. With the palm vertical to the ground, the wrist is bent upwards, bringing the thumb towards the forearm.

BOAST
A shot which hits the side wall before hitting the front wall (see page 65).

FLAT RACKET FACE
The racket face is vertical to the ground when the ball is struck.

OPEN RACKET FACE
The position used for most strokes with the higher edge of the racket face slightly behind the lower edge when the ball is struck.

CLOSED RACKET FACE
Opposite position to the open racket, with the top edge of the racket face slightly in front of the lower edge.

Gamal Awad from Egypt boasts with a 'flat' racket face against Australia's Dean Williams

(Above) Qamar Zaman commands the 'T' against Hiddy Jahan
(Below) Geoff Williams shows an 'open' racket face for a backhand shot

(Above) Dean Williams prepares to play a forehand with an 'open' racket face.
(Below) Karen Butterworth shows the 'cocked wrist' starting position for all strokes

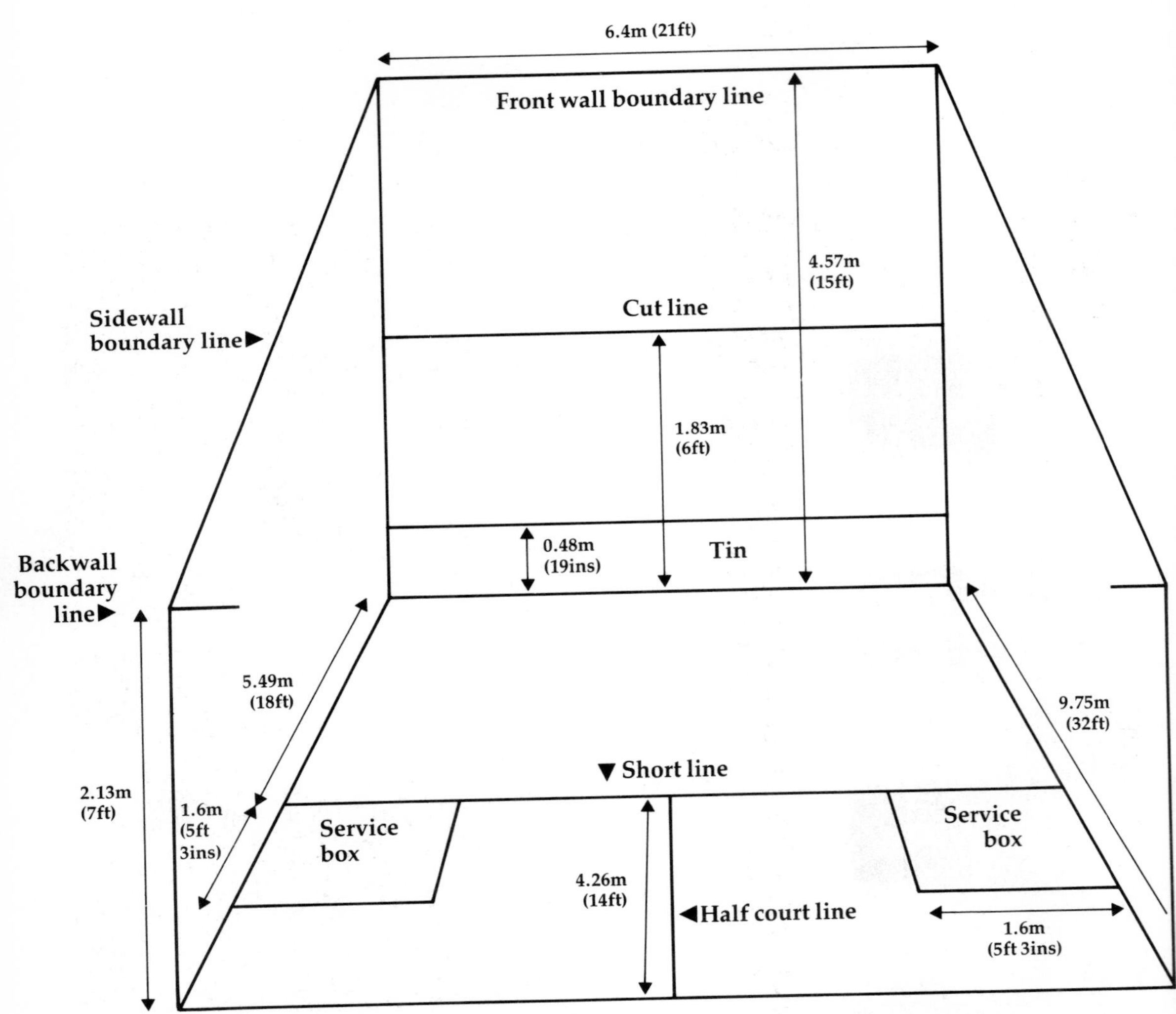

The dimensions of the squash court.

CUT
Slight backspin imparted to the ball through the use of an 'open' racket and high backswing.

CUT LINE ETC.
These lines on the floor and front wall of the court are shown in the diagram.

NICK
The junction between the wall and the floor. If the ball hits this, it fails to bounce and cannot be returned.

The perspex court (below) gives spectators all round the court a good view of the action

POSITION ON THE COURT

Before playing a shot you have to reach the ball. This will be much easier if you start from a good position and learn to move correctly to and away from the ball.

Basic position

The commanding position is the 'T', in the centre of the court and just behind the short line.

The experienced player varies this slightly to allow for the speed of the court and the opponent's position. Stand further back on a warm court when the ball tends to bounce further and higher. Come further forward on a cold court, when the ball will be much slower.

Your position should also be varied by moving slightly towards your opponent to enable you to pick up the next shot more easily.

Adopting a slight crouch with the knees a little bent allows you to move away quickly in any direction. Between shots try to hold your racket with the head slightly higher than your hand so that no time is wasted in starting the stroke. Watch the ball and your opponent hitting it. You can then anticipate the next shot and know where you will have to move.

Basic 'T' position

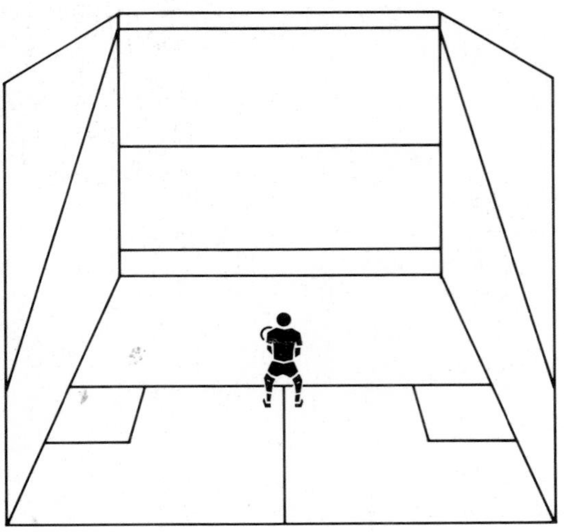

Lucy Soutter is ready to move from a slightly crouched position on the 'T'

MOVEMENT TO THE BALL

Movement from the basic position is not strictly to the ball, but to a point about three feet (one metre) to the side of the ball. This gives you a choice of shots to play and room to play them.

You can see from the diagram that this is best achieved by a movement which starts down the centre of the court and then goes towards the forehand or backhand side.

Large strides enable you to reach the ball quickly, with time to stop in a balanced position to hit it. A well balanced position and an accurate shot are most easily achieved by using the orthodox footwork shown in the pictures of the drives. Practise this until it becomes completely automatic.

Experienced players learn to play accurate shots off either foot, particularly on the forehand side at the back of the court. Provided your balance is good and your position is not cramped, this is often the best way to play the shot as movement away from the ball is then easier.

Movement to the ball

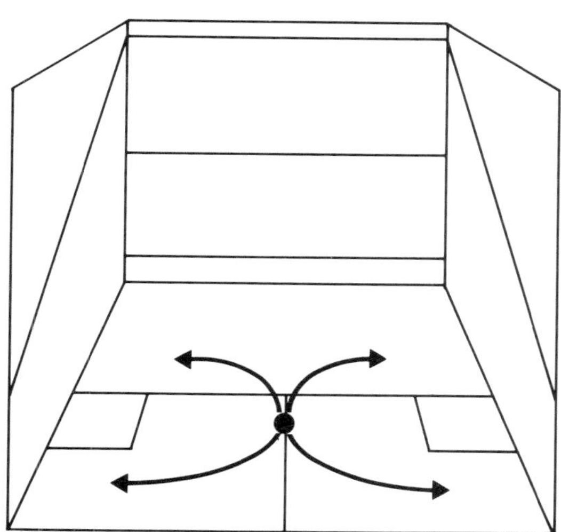

Jahangir Khan sets off at speed from the 'T'

MOVEMENT AWAY FROM THE BALL

You must allow your opponent a direct path to the ball and a clear hit to the front wall. Your movement away from the ball must allow this and also enable you to keep the ball in view the whole time.

After playing a good length shot from behind the service box, the best route back to the 'T' is behind your opponent.

If your starting position is further forward, you should try to move away in front of your opponent to reach the 'T'. Provided your own shot goes to a good length and stays near the side wall, you should have no problem. Remember your opponent may want to come across and volley and you must give him room.

From the front of the court, your movement needs to be slightly forward and then to the centre of the court.

Movement away from the ball

b) After length shot from near short line

a) After length shot from behind service box

c) After length shot from front of court

Dean Williams moves away from the ball and back to the 'T'

GRIP

There is little time in squash to change the grip, so it is essential to have a grip which can be used for all the different strokes.

To get the correct grip, hold the racket in your left hand with the head vertical. Then with your right hand shake hands with the handle, so that your thumb overlaps the second finger across the back. The first finger is placed rather like a 'trigger' finger on a pistol to give good racket head control. The end result looking down at your hand should be a pronounced 'V' between the first finger and thumb, with the point of the 'V' lined up with the left-hand corner of the shaft.

The end of the racket handle is usually slightly raised and this raised end should rest comfortably against the heel of your hand.

The 'shake hands' grip showing the 'V' between thumb and first finger

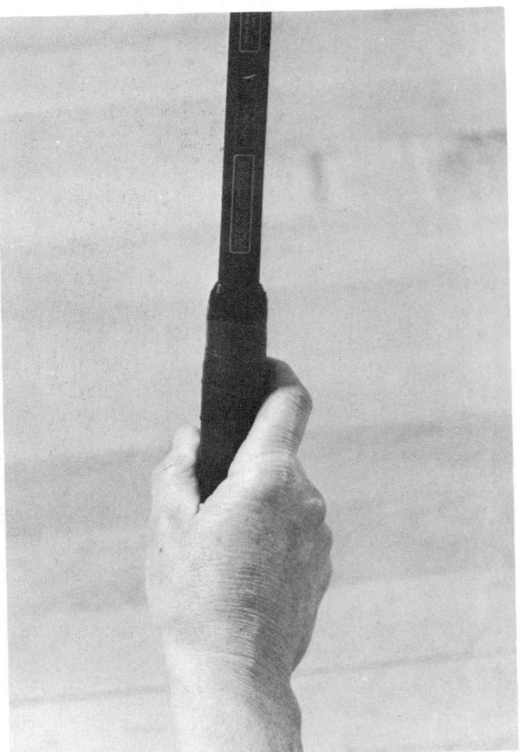

Front view of the grip shows the thumb overlapping the second finger

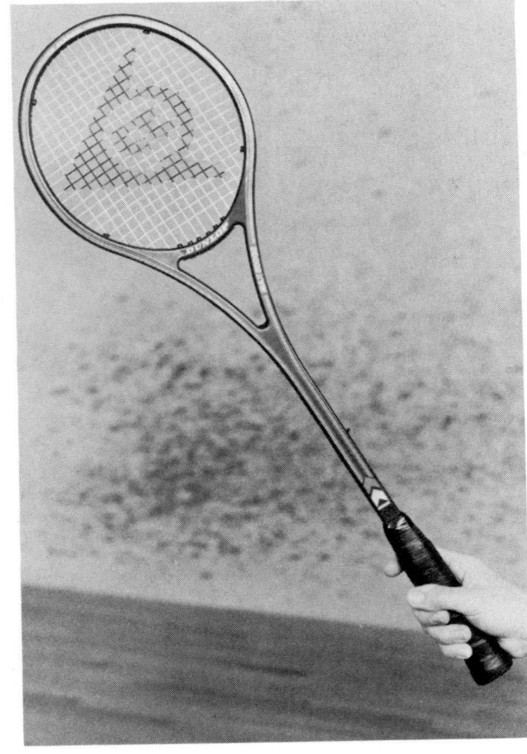

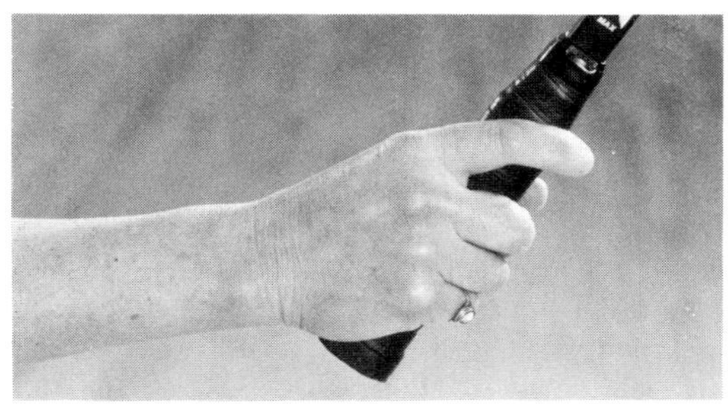

Back view of the grip shows the gap between first two fingers and the butt end resting comfortably against the heel of the hand

(Left) The grip in action on the forehand shown by Egypt's Ahmed Safwat
(Above) Ross Norman of New Zealand shows the same grip for the backhand

FOREHAND DRIVE

The straight length drive, keeping close to the side wall and played to a good length, is the basic shot of the game. The forehand swing is essentially a throwing action, similar to the one used to skim stones across a pond or throw a low fast ball.

To make the stroke easier to describe, we can break it down into its three key elements of backswing, hit through the ball, and follow through. Always keep in mind a picture of the whole stroke and try to copy from a good player.

Backswing

The backswing starts as your opponent's shot hits the front wall and you move to a position a few feet (a metre or so) to the side of the spot where you expect to hit the ball.

Lift the racket head high with the elbow bent and the wrist cocked.

At the top of the backswing the body weight is largely on the right leg, the feet are pointing to the side wall and the shoulders turned towards the back corner.

1

Hit through the ball

The hit through the ball starts with a step towards the side wall and a shift of weight to the left foot. The knee is bent to achieve a low, balanced position on impact with the ball.

The cocked wrist ensures that the racket head is well behind the hand as the elbow leads the swing through the ball.

The elbow is only straightened at the

2

moment of impact with the ball, which ideally is opposite the left knee and a comfortable distance away.

With the correct grip, the racket head should be slightly 'open', imparting some 'cut' to the ball.

Follow through

Balance must be maintained on the follow through, with the weight on the left leg and at least the toe of the back foot staying in contact with the ground behind you. The right shoulder stays low and the arm should bend quite naturally as the hand comes round to finish near the left shoulder.

Forehand drive demonstrated by New Zealand coach Ian McKenzie
The sequence shows the backswing, hitting through the ball and the follow through

5

3

4

BACKHAND DRIVE

The backhand swing is much the same as the forehand swing played backwards. The movement resembles the action used to throw a rubber ring onto a peg.

Backswing

As you move towards a point some feet (a metre or so) to the side of the spot where you expect to hit the ball, the racket is taken back and up with the wrist cocked and the elbow bent so that the racket head is above the left shoulder.

Using both hands to take the racket back helps to ensure a good turn of the shoulders. The left hand should then be left behind on the hit through the ball.

At the top of the backswing, the shoulders are turned towards the back corner, so that the right shoulder blade faces the front wall.

Hit through the ball

Start with a step onto the right foot and towards the side wall, with the knee bent.

The elbow leads the downward swing with the racket head staying behind the hand, until the arm is straightened on impact with the ball.

The correct grip keeps the racket head slightly open and the ball should be struck a comfortable distance away and just ahead of the right knee. The racket head must go through and not slice under the ball.

Backhand drive demonstrated by Lucy Soutter: backswing (with a two-handed start), hitting through the ball, and follow through

1

2

6

7

Follow through

The balanced position at impact is held in the follow through, with the left toe keeping in contact with the ground behind you.

The elbow bends on the follow through to take the racket head high and safely out of the way of your opponent.

3

4

5

Del Harris keeps his eye on the ball

Faults, causes and corrections

FAULT	CAUSE	CORRECTION
Missing or mis-hitting the ball	Not watching the ball	Watch and try to hit back of ball
Shot goes cross court	Facing front wall at impact	Turn more on backswing and keep sideways position on impact
	Ball hit too far forward	Wait or move forward to hit ball opposite front knee
	Racket head in front of hand at impact	Keep wrist cocked and racket strings facing front wall at impact
Ball hits side wall before reaching front wall	Ball hit too far behind front knee	Start stroke earlier or swing faster
	Racket head behind hand on impact, with wrist bent backwards	Keep wrist cocked and check grip. Make racket head go through the ball on impact
Excessive and dangerous backswing or follow through	Arm straight on backswing or follow through	Bend elbow on backswing and follow through to take racket head high. It should be possible to play the complete stroke with your back foot against the wall, then you can be sure that your swing presents no danger to your opponent
Weak shot because of excessive slice	Incorrect grip	Check and maintain correct grip
	Racket head stays behind hand on impact	Bring racket head through towards front wall on impact
Ball often hits tin or too low on front wall to get good length	Failure to appreciate that tin is not a net to be skimmed over	Aim higher
	Racket face closed on impact	Check grip. Keep racket strings facing front wall on impact

CROSSCOURT DRIVE

The technique for crosscourt drives is the same as for the straight drive, except that the ball is hit when it is further forward. The ball is aimed to hit the side wall just behind the back of the service box.

The danger of the crosscourt shot is that it goes through the middle of the court. Your opponent may cut it off here if he is in a good position and the ball is not played wide enough.

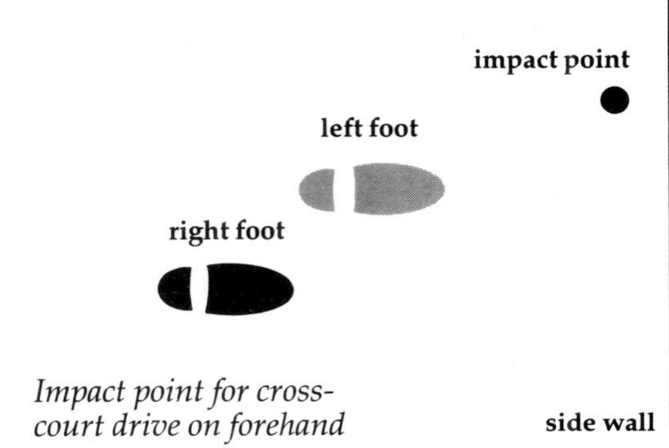

Impact point for cross-court drive on forehand

Practice

Hitting the same shot as often as possible is the only way to improve your accuracy and consistency. Fortunately in squash you can do quite a lot of practice on your own. Ideally you should find a partner of about the same standard to work on sequences of shots. Set yourself targets of length and width and number of shots and try to improve on these over a period of time.

SOLO

1 Count the shots in a rally to yourself down the side wall. Start by keeping your shots in half the court, progress to using the width of the service box and finally chalk a line parallel to the side wall to form a corridor for your drives. A corridor the width of six floor boards should be your ultimate aim.

2 Vary the height of your shots by playing them alternately above and then below the 'cut' line.

3 Try to land all your shots in the service box.

4 Try to land all your shots in the rectangle behind the service box.

PAIRS

1 Player 'A' hits or throws a gentle shot which drops about six feet (2 metres) from

Boast and drive

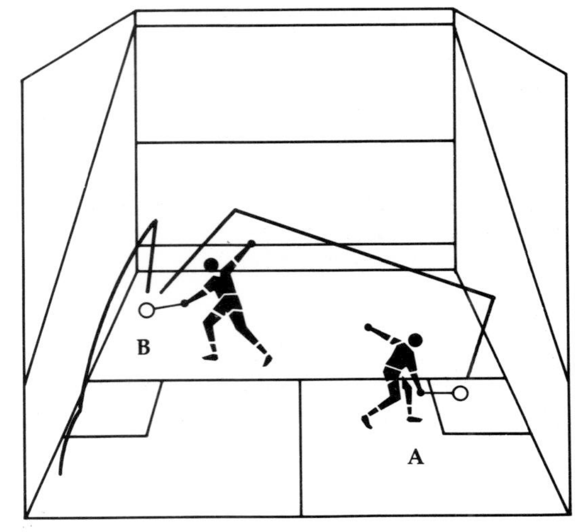

the front wall and quite close to the side wall. Player 'B' tries to hit a perfect length drive (second bounce very close to the back wall).

2 Have a rally with your partner in one half(side) of the court. Try playing all the shots behind the 'short' line. Make this more difficult by using a corridor the width of the service box or less.

3 Boast (see page 65) and drive. Player 'A' boasts, player 'B' drives straight, player 'A' boasts, player 'B' drives straight, etc.

4 Boast and two drives. Player 'A' drives straight, player 'B' drives straight, player 'A' boasts, player 'B' drives straight, etc.

5 Boast, crosscourt, straight. Player 'A' drives straight, player 'B' boasts, player 'A' drives crosscourt, player 'B' drives straight, etc.

6 Boast and varied drive. Player 'A' drives straight or crosscourt, player 'B' boasts, etc.

7 Drive and volley. Player 'A' stands on the 'T' and tries to volley or drive all shots to a length, player 'B' tries to get the ball past his partner along the side wall.

8 Boast and crosscourt drive. Player 'A' boasts, player 'B' plays crosscourt drive, player 'A' boasts, etc.

All these practices can be scored and played as a game by defining the area in which the drives must land.

THREES

1 Straight drives with two balls. Player 'A' on the forehand side, hits or throws a gentle shot which lands about six feet (two

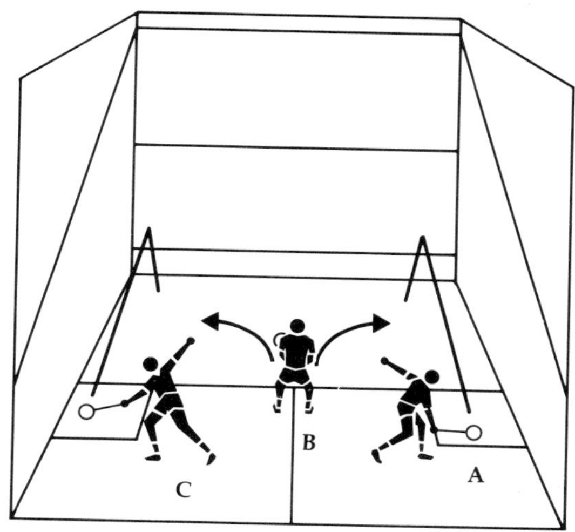

Straight drives with two balls

metres) from the front wall and near the side wall. Player 'B' drives straight, player 'C' hits or throws a gentle short ball on the backhand side, player 'B' drives straight, etc. Set a time and see who can hit most drives into a target area.

2 Straight drives with one ball. Player 'A' always drives straight, player 'B' stands behind the forehand service box, player 'C' stands behind the backhand service box. Both these players can boast or drop as they choose.

GAMES

1 Player 'A' plays normal game, player 'B' plays only length shots.

2 Player 'A' plays normal game, player 'B' drives straight down nearest side wall.

VOLLEY

The volley (hitting the ball before it touches the ground) is the best way to return service. It also puts more pressure on your opponent, giving him less time to reach the ball. The shot has the added bonus that you are cutting the ball off in mid-court and therefore retaining the commanding position near the 'T'.

Only the straight volley to a good length is covered in this section.

Backswing

If there is time, you should use the same sideways stance and footwork as for the forehand and backhand drives.

The backswing is short, with the racket lifted up and back.

The wrist is cocked, keeping the racket head above the hand.

Bend the elbow and use your forearm to take the racket head back so that the racket is almost parallel to the ground.

Hit through the ball

Good balance with the feet on the ground throughout the stroke is vital to ensure accuracy and consistency in the volley.

The arm comes forward in a 'punchy' action to hit the ball a comfortable distance away from the body and opposite the leading shoulder.

The racket face is kept slightly 'open', to hit the ball fairly high on the front wall.

Forehand volley – Backswing

Follow through

The follow through is short, with the racket head going through towards the point on the front wall where the ball is aimed.

Maintain the balance, keeping the back foot just in contact with the ground until the follow through is completed.

Forehand volley – hitting through the ball and follow through

The forceful volley of Susan Devoy keeps the pressure on her opponents

Backhand volley – backswing, hitting through the ball and follow through

Faults, causes and corrections

FAULT	CAUSE	CORRECTION
Missing or mis-hitting the ball	Not watching the ball	Look at underside of ball and try to hit it
Ball hits side wall before front wall	Impact point too far back	Hit ball earlier
Backhand volley hits side wall before front	Wrist bent so that back of hand faces side wall	Keep back of hand always facing front wall
Ball goes cross court	Impact point too far ahead	Wait and hit ball opposite leading shoulder
	Body swings round	Keep back foot on the ground
Failure to get good length	Aiming too low	Hit higher
	Racket face closed	Look at and hit underside of ball. Keep racket face 'open'.

Crosscourt volley

The technique is the same as for the straight volley, except that the ball is hit further in front of the body.

The ball is aimed to hit the side wall just behind the back line of the service box.

The ball must be played wide of your opponent if he is in the centre of the court, so that he cannot cut it off with an easy volley.

Practice

SOLO

1 Volley rally from close to the wall (six feet/two metres), to keep the stroke short.

2 Volley rally, moving one large step further away from the wall after each rally of six shots.

3 Volley rally, moving across the court along the 'short' line. Start on the forehand side and play backhand volleys, moving backwards until you reach the backhand side. Turn round and play forehand volleys back to your starting position.

4 Round-the-clock volleys. From fairly close to the wall, hit first one forehand and one backhand, then two forehands and two backhands, up to five each side. Then reverse the process until you get back to one volley on each side.

5 Corner volleys. Stand opposite one front corner of the court and rally first a forehand from front wall to side wall and return a backhand from side wall to front wall, etc.

PAIRS

1 Player 'A' hits a high shot from the back of the court, player 'B' volleys straight. Continue rally.

2 Player 'A' serves, player 'B' volleys straight.

3 Player 'A' hits high crosscourt, player 'B' volleys straight. Continue rally.

4 Crosscourt volley game. Players stand one in each back quarter of the court. The players volley to each other. Play this as a game, losing a point if you fail to return a ball which drops in your back quarter, or if your shot goes out of court or fails to reach the opposite back quarter.

5 Boast, crosscourt lob, straight volley. Player 'A' boasts, player 'B' lobs cross court, player 'A' volleys straight, etc.

6 Player 'A' hits high crosscourt or straight shot, player 'B' tries to cut all shots off with straight volley.

All these practices can be scored by defining the area in which the volley must land.

THREES

1 Straight volleys with two balls. Player 'A' hits high straight shot, player 'B' volleys straight, player 'C' hits high straight shot, player 'B' volleys straight. Set a time and score the number of volleys into a target area.

2 Straight volleys with one ball. Players 'A' and 'C' stand one in each back quarter of the court and hit high straight or crosscourt shots. Player 'B' tries to cut all shots off with a straight volley.

GAMES

1 Play a normal game but score a bonus point if you can win the rally with a volley.

2 Player 'A' plays a normal game, player 'B' must not allow any ball to hit the back wall.

SERVICE

There are many types of service but the two most commonly used are the high lob and the hard low service.

The aim of the service is to put your opponent on the defensive. Then he cannot attack the service without playing a risky shot. Occasionally you may even win the point outright.

The high lob service is very effective in most situations, but there are times when the low hard service is safer or more effective, and these are as follows:

1 Against an opponent with a very good volley who plays short volley winners off your high lob service.

2 On a court with a low ceiling or beams where the lob cannot be played high enough to be effective.

3 On a sweating court, where the condensation on the walls causes the high lob to skid upwards and go out of court on the front or side wall.

4 As a surprise, or after a long and exhausting rally, when the hard service to the side wall, straight at your opponent or to his backhand side, may catch him off balance.

5 At game or match ball when you are tense and fear that you may lob out of court.

6 If you know that your opponent dislikes a fast shot.

High lob service

The technique of the stroke is less important than where the ball goes.

The serve should be aimed to hit the front wall high, then touch the side wall above head height and just behind the back line of the service box, dropping gently to the floor at the back of the court.

BACKSWING

The rules of the game dictate that one foot has to be on the floor and inside the lines of the service box when the ball is struck.

Tactics dictate that your next move should be to the commanding position on the 'T'. Therefore the other foot is best placed in a comfortable position outside the box and towards the 'T'.

For a comfortable starting position, line up your hips and shoulders with the direction of the service.

Always watch your opponent to check on his position, in case he has moved forward to try and cut the serve off early.

Hold the ball in your left hand with the arm stretched comfortably out in front of you, then toss it up (not too high). At the same time, take the racket back to a position similar to that used to volley but rather lower.

HIT THROUGH THE BALL

Aim to hit the underside of the ball with the racket face 'open' so that it goes high on the front wall. Your aiming point on the front wall will depend on which side you are serving from.

From the right hand service box Aim to hit the front wall just to the right of the centre and well above the 'cut' line. You will need to experiment with your serve to find the best point to aim at, as this will vary according to your service action.

From the left hand service box The angle is different and you need to aim well to the right of the centre of the front wall to reach the desired spot on the side wall. The high lob is difficult to keep in court from this side. It is probably better to aim for a lower trajectory and rely on the flatter angle and closeness to the side wall to make the return difficult.

FOLLOW THROUGH

Because the shot is a fairly gentle one, the follow through is short but should take the racket head towards the point on the front wall where you have aimed the ball.

High lob serve from right hand service box

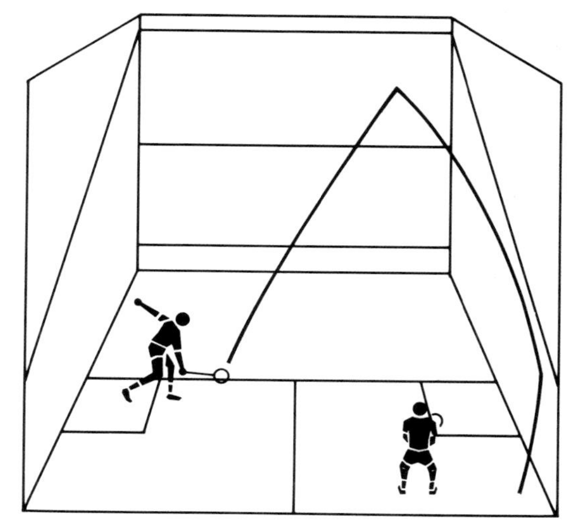

High lob serve from left hand service box

High lob serves showing backswing, hitting through the ball and follow through

(Right) From the right hand service box

(Below) From the left hand service box

Low hard service

This service is aimed to hit the front wall just above the 'cut' line and then touch the side wall just behind the service box and about eighteen inches (half metre) from the floor. This trajectory should take the ball to a good length at the back of the court.

BACKSWING

Assume the same starting position that you use for the lob serve so your opponent has no advance notice of your intention to serve hard. Toss the ball about head high, a comfortable arm's length away and slightly in front of you. Take the racket back at about shoulder level, with the racket head higher than your hand.

HIT THROUGH THE BALL

From the left hand box Give the ball a good thump, aiming to hit the front wall just above the 'cut' line and about half way between the centre and the right hand side wall.

From the right hand box The action is the same and the ball is aimed to hit the centre of the front wall just above the 'cut' line.

Low hard serve from left hand service box – backswing and hitting through the ball

Low hard serve from right hand service box – backswing, hitting through the ball and follow through

FOLLOW THROUGH

The follow through should take the racket head towards the point on the front wall where the ball is aimed. After you have served, move immediately to the 'T'. Remember to watch the receiver hit the ball so that you can anticipate the return.

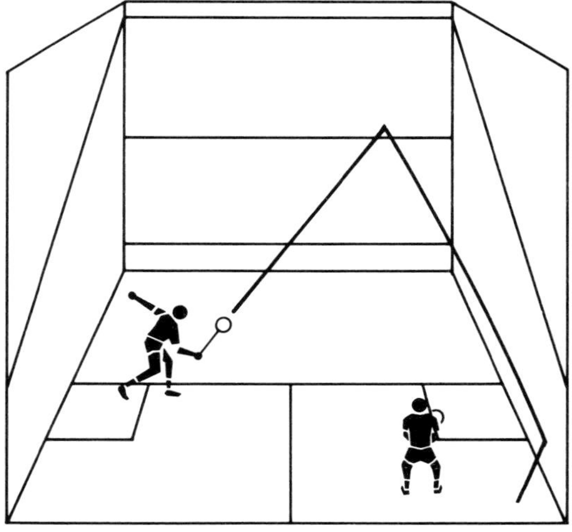

Low hard serve from left hand service box

Low hard serve from right hand service box

HARD SERVICE VARIATIONS

1 From the left hand service box, a hard low service aimed at the right hander's backhand side can be very effective. This must go to a good length as it is played almost down the centre of the court.

2 From either side a hard service aimed straight at the receiver can be very difficult to return. This should be aimed for the 'nick' at the back of the court.

Faults, causes and corrections

High lob service

FAULT	CAUSE	CORRECTION
Missing or mis-hitting the ball and failure to reach the front wall	Too long a backswing	Start with racket and ball close together and do not take racket far away from ball
	Poor hand/eye co-ordination	Practise close to the wall, moving back gradually
	Not watching the ball	Watch and try to hit the underside of the ball
Lack of height, giving an easy volley	Wrong grip with 'closed' racket face	Check grip and keep wrist 'cocked'
	Not hitting underside of ball	Watch and hit underside of ball
Ball goes out on side wall	Wrong angle	Check aiming point on front wall
	Hitting too hard, so ball still rising as it reaches side wall	Hit gently up through the ball so that it is dropping as it hits the side wall
Failure to touch side wall	Wrong angle	Check aiming point on front wall

Low hard service

FAULT	CAUSE	CORRECTION
Too high, giving easy volley	Hitting upwards, rather than through ball	Hit through, with racket head going towards aiming point just above 'cut' line
	Ball not thrown high enough	Throw ball up to head height
Hitting side wall too soon and coming into centre court Hitting side wall too far back, giving easy volley	Wrong angle	Check aiming point on front wall

Practice

1 Target practice, aiming at wall targets appropriate to the serve. (Stick a piece of paper on the side wall with 'Blutack'.) As a competition, score one point if the serve takes its first bounce in the area behind the service box. Score two points if the service also touches the side wall. Score three points if the serve hits the target.
2 Serve and then try to return the service with a boast.

RETURN OF SERVICE

The aim in returning service is to move your opponent from his position in the middle of the court and into the back corner.

The safest way to do this is with a straight shot close to the side wall to a good length. Ideally you should try to volley the ball before it hits the side wall.

If the service is a bit short, you should be able to play a drive.

The overhit service which comes some way off the back wall can also be returned with a drive.

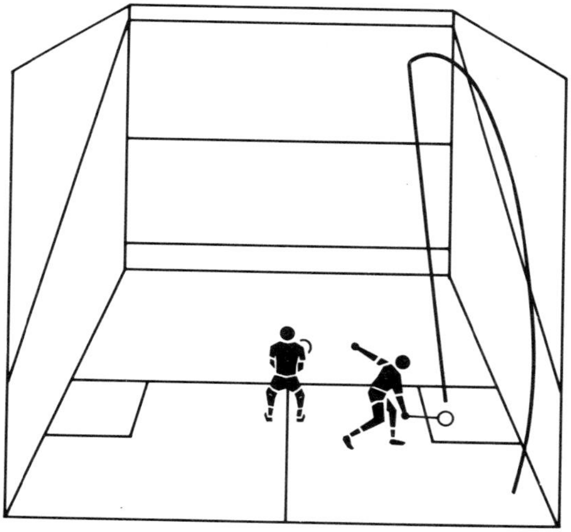

Straight length return of serve

The best position for the receiver is to stand about a racket length behind the back corner of the service box.

Face the nearest front corner, but watch

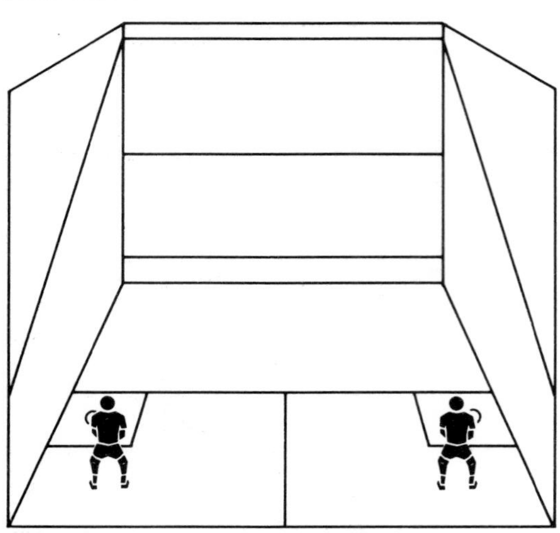

Received position

the server in case the service is an unexpected one straight at you or down the middle of the court.

The racket head should be kept well up, anticipating the volley return.

After returning the service, always return to the 'T', but watch the ball in case it comes towards the centre of the court. Always remember that your opponent must have a clear hit to the front wall and the side wall near the front wall. Otherwise you may give away a 'let' or 'stroke'.

Alternative service returns

Should the server move too far across, perhaps anticipating your standard straight return, or if the service is a poor one, there are a number of other effective returns.

Waiting to receive serve on the backhand side

CROSSCOURT LENGTH
The crosscourt lob or low length shot can be played on the same line as the service itself, aiming to hit the side wall just behind the service box and go to a good length.

Crosscourt length

Straight or crosscourt drop

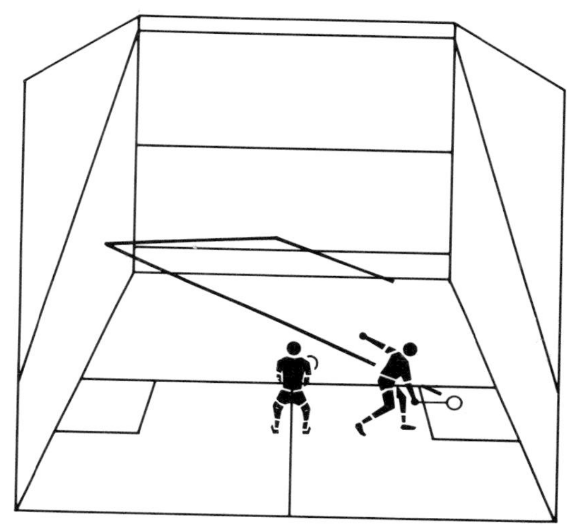

Reverse angle

Boast return of serve

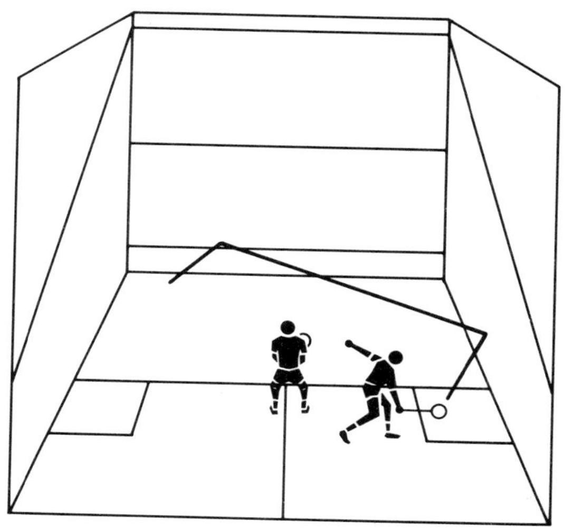

STRAIGHT OR CROSSCOURT DROP

If the service is a poor one, you may be able to attack it with a drop, played either on the volley or after the ball has bounced.

REVERSE ANGLE

This shot, aimed to hit the opposite side wall and finish near the front wall, close to the near side wall, can be a very effective return to a serve which is too short and comes some way off the side wall.

BOAST

The only return to a very good service may well be a boast or volley boast. This should hit the near side wall, finishing close to the front wall and near the opposite side wall.

The boast may also be used as a surprise return to attack a poor service.

Faults, causes and corrections

The faults are those which apply to the shot chosen as the return of service.

Remember that in a match your first priority is to return the ball on to the front wall somewhere. Otherwise your opponent wins an easy point.

Practice

1 In pairs, with each player having ten services. The server scores one point if the receiver fails to return the ball. The receiver scores a point if the return is a winner or the service is out of court. Neither player scores if the service is returned and the server can reply with a good return. Many of the practices described in the sections on drives and volleys can be used to practise the return of service by starting them with a service. The following are the most useful.

2 Drive and volley. Player 'A' serves, player 'B' drives or volleys straight. Continue the sequence with player 'A' trying to get the ball past his partner along the side wall and player 'B' driving or volleying straight.

3 Boast and cross court drive. Player 'A' serves, player 'B' boasts and sequence continues with player 'A' hitting crosscourt shots and player 'B' boasting.

4 Player 'A' serves, player 'B' volleys straight and sequence continues with player 'A' hitting high crosscourt shots and player 'B' volleying straight.

5 Boast, crosscourt, straight. Player 'A' serves, player 'B' volleys straight, player 'A' boasts and sequence continues with player 'B' hitting high crosscourt, etc.

6 Varied straight and crosscourt. Player 'A' serves, player 'B' volleys straight and sequence continues with player 'A' hitting straight or crosscourt high shots and player 'B' trying to cut all shots off with a straight volley.

BOAST

The boast hits the side wall nearest to you, then the front wall low, and finishes up in the opposite front corner of the court.

The perfect boast goes into the 'nick' but a very good one takes its second bounce just before reaching the opposite side wall and finishes close to the front wall.

The boast can be used as an attacking shot, played from around the 'short' line with your opponent behind you, or as a defensive shot to return a ball from deep in the back corners of the court.

Both these shots are described in more detail in the section on attacking shots, but the basic technique of the boast played from around the 'short' line is as follows.

Susan Devoy demonstrates a good shoulder turn for the forehand boast

Australian Glen Brumby makes a very full turn for the backhand boast

Backswing

The position and swing are the same as for the drive, because this gives no advance notice of your intention to boast.

Hit through the ball

Some players like to hit the shot with an 'open' racket face, so that the ball comes slowly down off the front wall and dies on the floor, while others prefer a faster shot with a 'flat' racket face.

The method you use depends on the tactical situation and on which you naturally play best. Whichever method is used, the impact point is slightly later than the drive, with the ball being struck a comfortable distance away and fractionally behind the leading foot.

You need to hit the ball up on the side wall, so that it is going downwards when it reaches the front wall. The ball should be aimed to hit the side wall about a foot or two ahead of the leading leg and about knee height.

Follow through

Follow through high, keeping the back foot touching the ground until the stroke is completed, to maintain your balance.

1

2

Backhand boast – backswing, hitting through the ball and follow through

3

4

5

Defeat and victory. Susan Devoy wins the 1985 British Open final against Martine le Moignan.

Faults, causes and corrections

Some of the faults covered under drives also apply to boasts, e.g. missing or mis-hitting the ball. Excessive or dangerous backswing or follow through. Weak shot with excessive slice.

FAULT	CAUSE	CORRECTION
Failure to reach the front wall	Wrong angle, because impact point too far behind leading foot	Check angle needed to reach front wall. Hit ball earlier
	Ball too low	Hit ball up the side wall
Ball comes into centre of court	Wrong angle, ball hitting side wall too far forward	Check angle needed to reach opposite front corner
	Too high, hitting front wall above 'cut' line	Hit lower on side wall, to reach front wall below 'cut' line
		Reduce power of shot

Practice

SOLO

1 Throw the ball on to the side wall (behind the short line) and hit the boast into a target area five to six feet (2 metres) from the front wall in the opposite front corner of the court.

2 Boast from behind the short line and run to return your own shot as a straight or crosscourt lob to the service box.

PAIRS

1 Boast and crosscourt. Player 'A' boasts, player 'B' hits crosscourt drive. Continue with player 'A' hitting boast, etc.

2 Boast and straight drive. Player 'A' boasts, player 'B' drives straight. Continue with player 'A' hitting boast, etc.

3 Boast and varied drive. Player 'A' always boasts, player 'B' drives straight or crosscourt.

4 Boast and two straight drives. Player 'A' boasts, player 'B' drives straight. Player 'A' drives straight, player 'B' boasts, etc.

5 Boast, crosscourt, straight. Player 'A' boasts, player 'B' drives crosscourt, player 'A' drives straight, etc.

6 Boast, drop, boast, drive. Player 'A' boasts, player 'B' plays a weak drop (just setting the ball up for his partner and not trying to play a winning shot), player 'A' boasts, player 'B' drives straight, etc.

All these practices can be scored by defining the target areas in which the ball must land.

GAME

Play a normal game but score a bonus point if you can win the rally with a boast.

PAUL WRIGHT

Part Three: Attacking and defensive shots

You will at some time reach a certain standard of play when, in order to improve, you will need to introduce some new shots into your game to give you greater variety and enable you to kill the ball more often. This section of the book is intended as a guide to help you increase your range of shots.

You will, of course, by this time have developed your own particular playing style which may be of a defensive or an aggressive attacking nature. It is preferable to strike a balance between the two, and hopefully this section will enable you to do so.

If you are a defensive player, you will need to learn how to finish off a rally successfully and how to play attacking shots which your opponent cannot retrieve. If you are an attacking player, you may need to learn to be patient and keep rallies going, only finishing them off with a winning shot when the circumstances are right. Always remember that mistakes can still be made even when you feel you are in a perfect position to play a winner. Attacking shots are always risky but much more exciting. When you have mastered some different shots you will find that you will get much more enjoyment from your game, not only because you are able to play better shots but also because you are able to retrieve you opponent's better shots.

Try to be versatile in your game so that when you are playing a match you use the early rallies to assess your opponent and to decide which type of game to play against him. Stay alert and ready to change the pattern as he may be doing the same to you.

I have tried to describe and illustrate the shots in this section in such a way that you can imagine yourself actually playing them on the court. There are other variations to these shots; I have only tried to give you the basic guidelines. But if you follow them you should have a reasonable amount of success. Remember, keep practising; and above all, winning or losing, enjoy your squash!

The ever versatile Qamar Zaman deceives the eyes with the speed of this shot.

Attacking shots

DROPSHOTS

Many players face the problem of not being able to kill the ball when the opportunity arises. Dropshots are a very good way of finishing a rally when your opponent has hit a loose shot.

Paul Wright plays a crosscourt drop with an open racket face and a short backswing. See how the racket comes up underneath the ball. It's vital to keep the knees and the back well bent and the eyes on the ball

THE CROSSCOURT DROPSHOT

As the name implies this shot is aimed diagonally from one side of the court low into the opposite front corner. There are two kinds of crosscourt dropshot which are very similar to one another but which serve different purposes.

The first could be described as a working dropshot; it is not necessarily aimed to finish the rally, but more to move your opponent forward, trying to force him to make a loose or poor return. The ball is played across the court, hitting the front wall low, fading at an angle on to the floor and then towards the adjacent side wall.

The second type is the 'nick dropshot', aimed at the gap between the side wall and the floor. This is an excellent shot with which to finish a rally and when played successfully can be exciting both to play and to watch. The ball should be aimed across court at such an angle towards the opposite front corner that it strikes the front wall above the tin, high enough to allow a margin for error, but low enough to produce an effective shot. Don't worry too much about aiming the ball just one

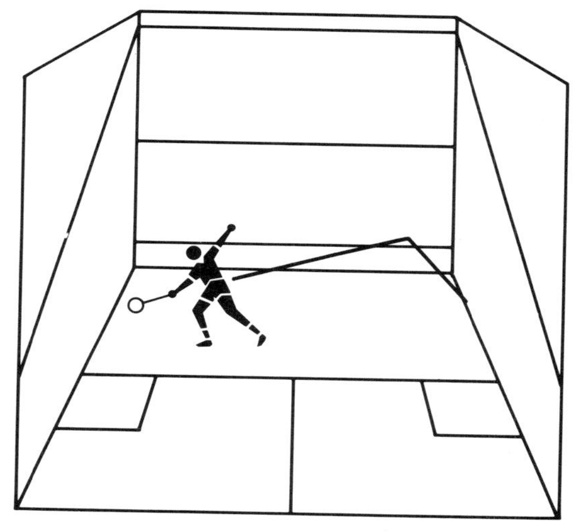

The target for the crosscourt drop: front wall, side wall, floor

inch (three cm) above the tin: you can strike as high as one foot (thirty cm) up the front wall and still produce a winning shot. But if the shot is not played accurately the ball will stand up too high and

Starting with a backswing, the cut dropshot is played with an open racket face, swung across the back of the ball to impart backspin

come back in towards the centre of the court. More important than the height is the angle at which the drop leaves the front wall and moves on to the next target, which is the side wall as near to the floor as possible.

Now that you know the targets to aim for with a crosscourt drop you must help the shot to work regularly by getting your position around the ball correct and making the swing and racket work to your advantage.

The swing

There are two ways of hitting the dropshot and it would be advisable to practise and use both equally well. Generally players find that they favour one shot more than the other and only develop that particular method.

The push dropshot swing

The first way of hitting the ball, which I call a push dropshot, is to take a very short backswing on the backhand, virtually no backswing on the forehand, then, presenting the racket face in an open position and using just the forearm opening from the elbow, keeping the wrist cocked, push the racket under the ball, making sure that the wrist stays firm throughout the stroke. The most important thing to remember is to keep the racket moving through after the point of impact with the ball. Do not let the ball just bounce off the racket strings. The follow through, even if only a short one, is vital to ensure accuracy.

The cut dropshot swing

The second way of hitting a dropshot is by cutting or slicing, which will put a certain amount of backspin on the ball. (Spin does not have such an effect on a squash ball as it has in tennis or table tennis, but it is, nevertheless, helpful in making the shot finish shorter and tighter.) Unlike the

push drop, a certain amount of backswing is needed for this shot on both forehand and backhand. You must make the stroke with the forearm opening out and the wrist in the cocked position. The racket face must be open but the swing for the cut drop must take a path across the back of the ball, thus imparting the backspin.

Remember to follow through. This will come more naturally with the cut drop as it has been started with a backswing.

The cut drop can be played with varying racket head speed from very slow to a fast aggressive cut across the back of the ball, whereas the push drop must be played slowly, with control. The cut drop, because of its backswing, can be used to deceive your opponent into thinking that you are about to drive the ball. The advantage of the push drop is that you do not need so much time to prepare to play it, but the disadvantage is that your intentions will be more obvious to your opponent. This will not matter too much as long as you keep the ball very tight into the front corners.

Position

As the drop you are about to play is to be aimed across court, the first thing you must do is to make sure that you are in a position to take the ball from in front of your leading foot. If you let the ball come level with or behind your leading foot you will find it very difficult indeed to play. (The 'leading foot' is the left foot on the right side of the court and the right foot on the left side.) The next thing to ensure is that you are in position not too close to the side walls or the back of the court. A high percentage of crosscourt drops are played from in front of the 'T'.

Make sure that when you approach the ball you are well balanced, as this will not only help you to strike the ball well but also allow you to move smoothly away after playing the stroke. Do not rush to play the shot, try to steady yourself first. It is not always necessary to be on the correct foot but is more important to be well balanced.

Try to get into a position where you could draw a line across your toes to the point where you want the ball to strike the front wall.

The ball is best taken at the top of its bounce or on the rise but it is hardest to take when it is falling. Keep your eye on the ball all the time, bend your back and knees to get down to a good level to strike the ball.

Practice

SOLO
Feed yourself a ball off the front wall so that it comes easily into the court and play either a backhand or forehand drop into the opposite front corner.

PAIRS
1 A good set practice is to play sidewall boast, crosscourt drop, straight drive, repeating the exercise and playing this as a game to see who can win the most points in a set time or with American scoring to a set number of points. With this practice you will also improve your straight drive return of a crosscourt dropshot, your playing of a boast from a drive and your movement around the court. You will also improve your fitness as a good deal of movement up and down the court is required. See if you can hit the nick.
2 Play a game where each time the ball lands in the front half of the court you must play either straight or crosscourt drops which must be retrieved by your partner and hit to length; and then the rally continues.

Jahangir Khan plays a straight cut drop in the 1986 British Open Final against Ross Norman

THE STRAIGHT DROPSHOT

The straight dropshot is the most important to be able to play. It may not make you so many winning points but is a very good way of putting your opponent into the front of the court, making him work hard for the ball and hopefully giving a poor return which you can move in and finish off.

Your aim should be to hit the ball straight into either the backhand or forehand front corner depending upon which side of the court you are on. Unlike the crosscourt drop, your target is to get the ball as tight to the side wall as possible, parallel with it and not coming back too far into the court. This makes the ball very difficult for your opponent to retrieve.

The straight dropshot can be used within a good range from right up close to the front of the court to about two thirds of the way back down the court, i.e. just behind the back line of either service box.

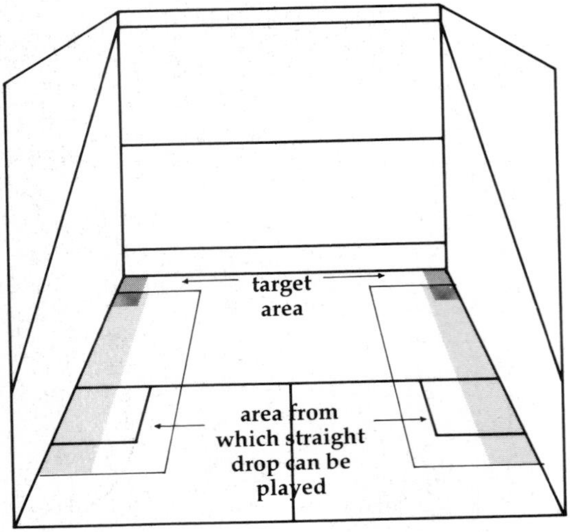

Be careful, because the further away from the front wall you are the more likely you are to make mistakes.

If you are presented with a ball that stands slightly out from the side wall, you can make an angle on your drop shot by turning your body slightly so that, when struck, the ball just touches the side wall before the floor and therefore finds the nick, instead of staying parallel with the side wall. This is more often possible in the front of the court. It is probably the drop used most frequently by the top players.

THE SWING

The method of striking the ball is the same as for the crosscourt dropshot. It can either be pushed with an open faced racket and a good follow through or cut with a shortened backswing going across the back of the ball.

(Right) David Pearson follows through after playing a straight drop against Gawain Briars

1

2

3

4

5

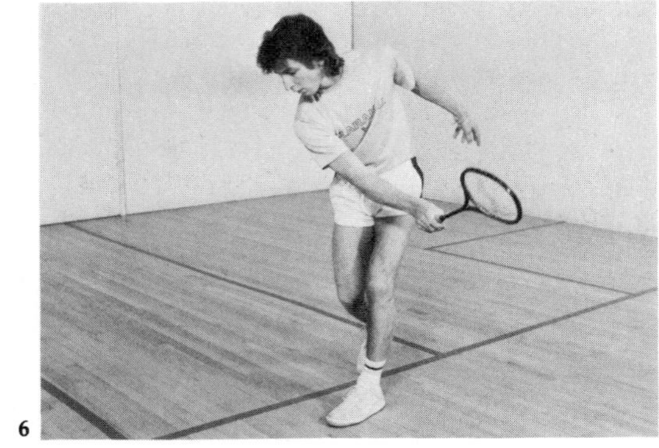
6

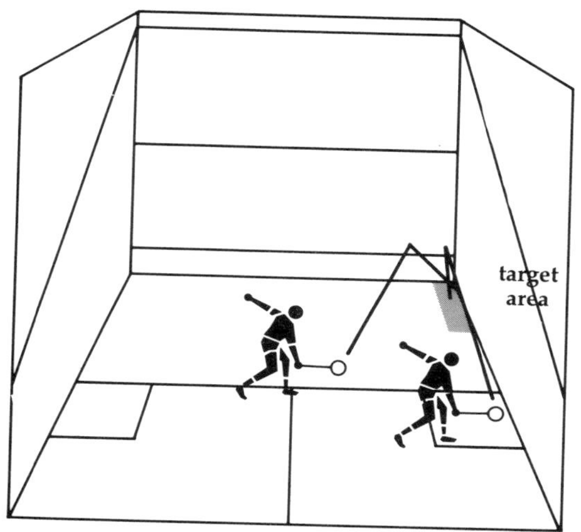

The target area for the straight push drop

Position

The ball is taken in a different position from the crosscourt drop. You must get yourself around the ball more, being ready to take it from level with or just in front of your leading foot. The shoulders are best positioned parallel to the side wall or, if the ball is away from the side wall, giving you an angle to work with, the leading shoulder pointing to where you are aiming the ball. The ball should be taken slightly earlier on the backhand than on the forehand. The advantage of playing a straight drop is that the ball is a lot tighter and most of the time you can make your opponent wait until you have played the stroke, by putting your body between him

(Opposite) The straight push drop is played with a short backswing and an open faced racket

and the ball, before he can move to retrieve it. This obviously gives you more time to recover and to retrieve his possibly rushed return. On the crosscourt drop he can anticipate the shot and move before you actually play the stroke. However, remember that after you have played the shot you should, according to Rule 12, give your opponent 'Fair View and Freedom of Stroke'. This means that he must be able to see the ball and to move in to retrieve the shot uninterrupted by you or your swing, therefore you must move off the ball and out of your opponent's way as quickly as possible.

Practice

SOLO

1 Feed yourself balls to varying lengths down the side walls and try to play the stroke either by pushing or cutting, aiming to keep the ball as short and as tight to the side walls as possible.

2 To practise the nick, feed the ball further away from the side walls short of or just behind the short line and play the shot with either cut or push into the front corners, angling the ball just to hit the side wall before the floor.

PAIRS

1 One of you can feed the ball from the front of the court, to various lengths, down the side walls while the other tries to play the drop as short and tight as possible.

2 Slightly advanced of this would be to play a rally down either side wall to a set routine of LONG, LONG, SHORT, which means that both players get equal turns at playing

1

a straight drop shot from a drive. This is another good fitness exercise.

3 To play straight or short angled drops from further forward, the best routine would be to play boast, straight drop, drive. You will have to do some quite hard

The straight cut drop showing the higher backswing and an open faced racket cutting across the ball

2

3

4

5

moving to keep this exercise going and also ensure that you are playing the shot in such a way that you allow your partner good access to retrieve your drop. This routine means that your partner will be playing drops on the opposite side of the court to you. I suggest that, unless you are working on one particular stroke, you change sides to enable you both to get practice at forehand and backhand drops.

POINTS TO REMEMBER ABOUT DROPSHOTS

1 Allow yourself a margin for error in height. Don't aim immediately above the tin, aim at least nine inches to one foot (25–30 cm) above.
2 Always follow through, if only slightly.
3 Make the stroke with your arm, not your wrist.
4 Bend your knees and back to get down to a good level with the ball, keep your eye on the ball and think of your target, i.e. front, side, floor, for the nick.
5 Play working dropshots as well as winning dropshots to expose your opponent at the front of the court.
6 After playing the shot, don't relax thinking that you have played a winner, always expect your opponent to retrieve the ball and you will not be caught out.
7 If you are at all doubtful about playing the shot then hit length; you will be less likely to make a mistake.
8 Keep your straight drops as short and tight to the side wall as possible.

Gamal Awad plays a straight drop against Jahangir Khan in the world's longest ever squash match (2 hours 46 minutes) – the Final of the 1983 Patrick International Squash Festival at Chichester

KILLS

Kills, using more power than dropshots, are another very effective way of finishing a rally when your opponent has hit a loose shot.

Straight kill

When played well, this shot looks very simple but can have a devastating effect. It is an excellent way to finish off a high bouncing loose ball from your opponent. It is best played from the front of the court.

The idea of the straight kill is to keep the ball parallel to the side wall but have it finish as quickly as possible. Although your target should be to hit the ball low on the front wall you must remember to allow yourself a margin for error as with the

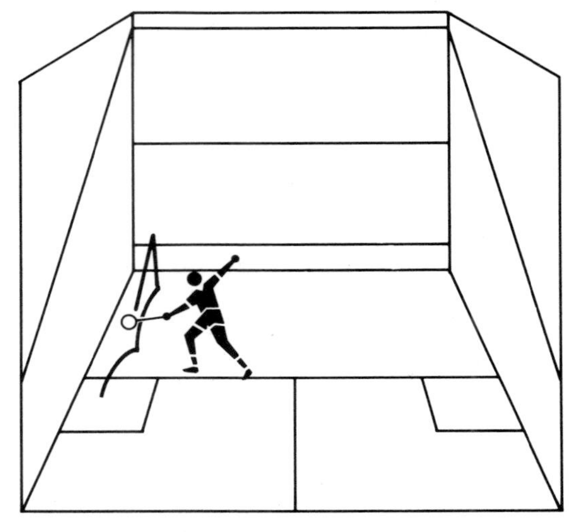

The target area for the straight kill

The straight kill is played low on the front wall keeping the ball parallel to the side wall. The ball must bounce twice, as quickly as possible.

dropshot. All too often I have been in a good position for this shot but then just caught the top of the tin, by not making enough allowance, and therefore lost the rally.

SWING AND POSITION

The position is exactly the same as for a normal straight drive. You strike the ball level with the leading foot and the shoulders facing the side wall. Have a well prepared backswing and with a firmly balanced stance get to the ball early, either when it is rising or at the top of its bounce.

To make the shot different from an ordinary drive you must change the way in which you actually strike the ball. The preparation is exactly the same as for a straight drive, with the racket lifted into a good backswing. The downswing must have plenty of power, lots of speed, and the racket face can be presented in one of two ways according to the bounce of the ball or in your own preferred striking method. It is obviously advantageous to be able to use both.

For the first method you need to take the ball at the top of its bounce, and this must be higher than the tin. Bring the racket down on to the ball with a slightly closed face as fast as you can without losing your balance. This will make the ball hit the front wall low and then bounce twice very quickly on the floor.

The second method of playing a straight kill is more often successful but technically a little harder. The target remains the same, preparation is exactly the same as for the first method, with the racket well raised into a good backswing. But you then swing the racket open faced across the back of the ball, cutting it so as to put a good deal of backspin on it. This will have the effect of holding the ball short and making it bounce twice very quickly. The advantage with this method is that because you are taking the ball with an open face it does not have to have such a high bounce as needed for the kill with the closed face racket. You can also vary the speed of the downswing, which will vary the pace of the shot.

Practice

SOLO

Set yourself an easy ball in the front of the court which bounces higher than the tin and is a yard or so away from the side wall. Then try to kill it straight, ideally so that it bounces twice before the short line.

PAIRS

One partner can feed an easy ball off the front wall to land before the short line, while the other practises short straight kills on either the forehand or backhand side of the court. If you wish to alternate sides the feeder can play a boast high on the front wall and his partner can continually try to kill each boast straight and short with either striking method as often as he can.

Crosscourt kill

This is a very good way of finishing off a loose ball left at the front of the court by your opponent. A good example would be either a drop played too high and not close

The crosscourt kill showing the high backswing. The ball is taken in front of the body and driven hard and low across the court.

enough to the side wall, or a defensive boast which stands up in the front of the court, again away from the side wall.

The idea of this shot is that you play the ball across court with power, to finish as quickly as possible by bouncing twice before the short line. Also, if possible, try to get the ball to travel towards the side wall, meeting it at about the service box. This is called getting it to a good width. The advantage here is that your opponent must move off the 'T' to have a chance of retrieving the shot and also, very often, you will find the nick on the side wall; whereas if you do not get good width on the shot you will never get the nick.

THE SWING

There are two ways of hitting the crosscourt kill. One way is to cut the ball, which I think is the best method, and the second is to hit it with a flat or closed faced racket. These methods can be used on both forehand and backhand.

When moving to the ball to cut the crosscourt kill you must have the racket prepared, get to the ball early and strike it at either the top of its bounce, which is the best time, or when it is on the rise. Do not take a falling ball or you will make too many errors. Bring the racket down in a fast sharp cutting swing across the back of the ball, aiming to hit the front wall low but with a margin for error. I would suggest nine inches to one foot (25–30 cm) above the tin. The ball should not rise at all after leaving the front wall and should travel low across the court, bouncing twice very quickly. (For those of you who have had the pleasure of watching Peter Marshall play, he uses this shot regularly and very effectively. Perhaps this is one of the advantages of being a two handed player.)

The second way of striking this shot is by using the racket face flat or slightly closed and hitting through the back of the ball, not across it, driving it once again downwards on to the front wall. Be very careful with this shot as it must only be played off a ball at the top of its bounce, which must be higher than the top of the tin. If it is not higher you will find yourself continually driving the ball into the tin. Try to use a nice fast swing to produce a quick powerful shot which dies across the court.

POSITION

To take advantage of loose balls played by your opponent you should be in a position to attack the ball either from the 'T' or moving forward having already read your opponent's shot and realizing his mistake.

The ball should be taken from in front of your leading foot and the body can either be positioned round towards the side wall or just slightly open with the weight being transferred from the back foot on to the front foot then on to the ball.

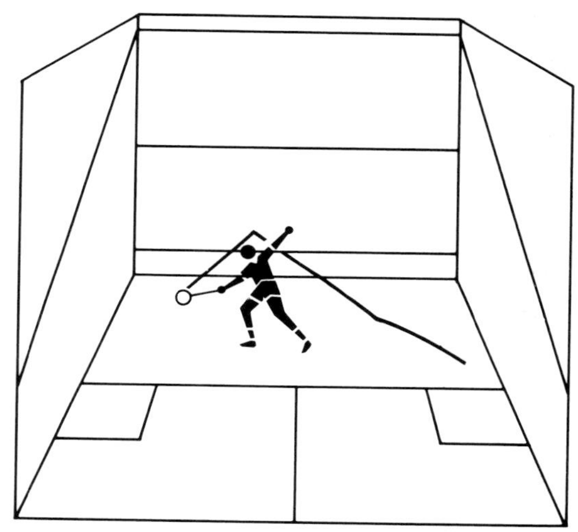

The target area for the crosscourt kill

It does very often pay to get just a little closer to the ball than normal as this then has the effect of keeping the ball low. However do not get too close or you will find the tin too often. After playing the shot make sure that you move quickly back to the 'T' in case your opponent should manage to return the kill. Do not assume that you have won the rally.

Practice

SOLO

Practising this stroke individually is not too easy as you cannot keep the ball going. The best way is to set yourself a high bouncing ball on the front wall, move to it

Peter Marshall, successful at a phenomenally early age, is one of the world's few two handed players

and play the crosscourt kill. You will then have to go and get the ball and feed yourself another high boast.

PAIRS
If you have a partner it is much easier. One plays a high soft boast to the front of the court from around the short line, while the other moves to and from the 'T' to the boast and tries to play crosscourt kills all the time. See how quickly you can make the ball die, experimenting with the stroke, cutting or striking through the ball.

POINTS TO REMEMBER ABOUT KILLS
1 Do not take the ball too late or when it is too close to either side wall.
2 When playing the shot do not try to hit it so hard that you turn your body or you will undoubtedly snatch the ball and hit the tin or send it too wide thus bringing it out down the middle of the court with yourself out of position.
3 Keep the ball down below the level of your opponent's knees on a downward path otherwise it will travel too far into the court and give your opponent a chance to leave you at the front with his return going to the back.

Volley kills

As you become a better player you will generally find that you will be looking to volley the ball more. That does not mean that you need to take the ball on the volley as often as the shot presents itself, but most top players will see the opportunity to volley and then decide whether or not it is possible to do so without losing control or if it is the right thing to do tactically.

For the two volley kills that follow you must remember that you are always taking a chance. Even if your opponent is well out of position and you are in a very good position you still risk making a mistake when playing this shot, whereas if you were simply to volley the ball to length the chances of making a mistake are much smaller.

These volley kills are very pleasing to play when they work as intended. You must remember, however, not to relax after playing them but to stay alert, because if your opponent is good he will be able to read them and possibly retrieve them.

Crosscourt nick volley

The crosscourt nick volley should be taken from an easy ball, preferably in an attacking position in the middle part of the court. The aim is to get the ball to take a crosscourt downward path into the front corners, either on the backhand or the forehand. You will obviously be aiming the ball to hit the front wall low, but be careful not to aim too low or you will make too many errors on an already risky shot. It is not the height on the front wall that makes the shot effective but the angle at which the ball strikes the front wall. The aim is to make the ball hit front wall, side wall, floor, and the lower you hit the side wall the better.

There are two types of nick: a 'plain nick' shot hits the front wall, then the side wall just before the floor, and the 'dead

nick' hits the front wall then the side wall and floor simultaneously.

SWING AND POSITION

Remember when taking volleys to prepare the racket head early. A common problem that many players have when trying to volley is that they do not prepare the racket early enough and therefore they play the ball too late.

You can use either an open faced racket or a closed faced racket for this shot. With the open faced racket you should cut across the back of the ball. You must remember to keep the wrist cocked on both forehand and backhand. Do not try to play the stroke using the wrist, keep it cocked all the way through. Take the ball from in front of the body, face around towards the side wall and make sure that the stroke is played with the arm. Try not to direct the ball by moving your upper body, make sure that when you strike the ball your grip is kept firm and that you continue the stroke with a good follow through.

This stroke can be played either aggressively, i.e. hit hard, or delicately, i.e. hit very soft, just finishing in either front corner.

When the stroke is played with a closed faced racket the difference is that you must get the racket head over the top of the ball, once again using the arm to make the stroke and not the wrist. The ball should still be taken from in front of the body. On the forehand you can open the stance up a little to get the ball into the angle around the front corner, but on the backhand you must stay facing the side wall.

Remember when playing this stroke that the ball must be in a relatively easy position in the middle third of the court, well away from the side walls. An example of this would be a bad crosscourt ball from your opponent, or a poor width and length service.

The crosscourt nick volley showing how the racket is prepared early. Keep your eye on the ball and use an open faced racket cutting across the back of the ball to bring it down into the front corner of the court

Practice

SOLO

Feed yourself a ball lifting off the front wall at a height around the short line which you can volley, then play the shot to your selected crosscourt front corner.

PAIRS

One of you can feed a bad crosscourt lob which the other can then volley towards the nick. Between the two of you play thirty feeds and count how many winning volleys are made and also how many hit the tin or the side wall first.

Straight volley kill

The straight volley kill can be used on a ball which is neither too high nor too tight to the side walls. It is usually an advantage to have your opponent behind you, although occasionally if he is not watching the ball or is slow moving forward it can be just as well to play the shot from behind him.

The straight volley kill can have two targets. One is to aim the ball low in a downwards direction, trying to keep it as tight and parallel to the side wall as possible. The other is to hit the front wall then the side wall very low. This is best used when you are taking the ball at an acute angle. It is possible here, as with the crosscourt shot, to hit the nick, aiming the ball to hit front wall, side wall, floor.

SWING AND POSITION

The racket must be prepared early with a short backswing. You must be well balanced, preferably moving forward on to the ball. The racket can be either closed faced over the ball or slightly open faced cutting the ball.

On either side of the court the ball should be taken slightly in front of the body and driven or cut downwards to hit the front wall fairly low and bounce twice on the floor as quickly as possible or, better still, hit the nick. My preference is to play this shot from over the ball with a closed faced racket and try to hit it reasonably hard so that it finishes quickly, bouncing twice as soon as possible.

Practice

SOLO

Set yourself about three feet (one metre) away from either of the side walls, near the short line. Feed yourself a ball to come from the front wall down the court at about head height, then play the straight volley kill. Try to return your shot as another feed so that you keep the practice going.

PAIRS

One partner feeds from the service box area while the other takes the volley from in front, trying to bring the ball down as sharply as possible with power.

If you wish to have a change of sides the feeder can play a boast every third shot which moves the ball across to the other side of the court. This is then driven, the feeder plays three more volleys on the opposite hand, then repeats with another boast.

POINTS TO REMEMBER ABOUT KILLS

1 Do not take a ball that is either too high or too tight to the wall.

2 Make sure that you are well balanced when playing the shot, either moving forward on to the volley or in a good position when the ball gets to you. Do not lunge out for the shot or overreach.

3 Keep your wrist tight. If you turn the wrist when playing the shot it will be inaccurate.

4 Try to keep the shoulders round towards the side wall, especially on the backhand.

5 Take the ball from slightly in front of the body, never late.

6 Think of the target that you want to hit, either straight and tight to the side wall or a narrow angle to hit the nick.

7 If you intend to volley make sure that you are fit as you are now playing the game at a faster pace. You will also be forcing your opponent to play at a faster pace which he may not like.

8 Do not be afraid of playing winners when the opportunity arises. You will enjoy the game more and anyone watching you will find it much more exciting.

ANGLE SHOTS

The main advantage of playing angle shots is that they can deceive your opponent, making him wrongfooted and unable to retrieve your ball whether or not it would have been an outright winner. But be careful: if your opponent is a good player and reads your angle shots well he can attack them with either hard drives or winning dropshots, leaving you in a poor position on the court.

There are three varieties of angle shot: the attacking boast, the short angle shot, and the reverse angle.

The attacking boast

The attacking boast can be played anywhere from about one third of the way back from the front wall all the way down

The attacking boast. The ball is taken behind the leading foot, with a flat or slightly open faced racket

the side wall into the back of the court. The best time to play it is when you are aware that your opponent is not watching the ball, thus catching him out, or when he is rather slow moving to the front of the court. If the shot is to succeed the ball must be away from the side wall and preferably not to a good length.

SWING AND POSITION

The shot should be played with your leading foot ahead of the ball (though if you are in trouble, you can play the forehand off the wrong foot quite successfully). Some players start with a very low short swing. However, for deceptive purposes, it is best to raise the racket as if you were going to play either a straight or a crosscourt drive. If the racket is left low you could perhaps make it appear that you are about to play a drop shot.

The racket face should be presented either flat or slightly open faced. Play the ball to hit the side wall as sharply as you can, not too far ahead of your body or you will send it back down the centre of the court. The ball should travel across court off the side wall, dropping down on to the front wall and finishing in the opposite front corner.

There are two shots you can aim for. One is the fading boast, when the ball fades gently across the court, falling from the front wall, bouncing no higher than the top of the tin and travelling towards the opposite side wall. This will force your opponent to play the return from under the ball.

The second target is the nick boast. This can be very effective when played well, as the ball finishes very quickly, but if it is played badly, either too high or with not enough angle, it tends to sit up in the front of the court or come back off the opposite side wall into the centre of the court, making an easy return for your opponent. With this shot your body must be well forward of the ball, allowing you to hit it very sharply on to the nearest side wall so that it travels across on to the front wall and, before hitting the floor, hits the opposite side wall as low as possible, hopefully finding the nick.

Quite a few top players, including Dean Williams, have become very successful with this boast. Others such as Ahmed Safwat favour the fading boast which is played more gently, stretching the opponent rather than being an outright winner.

Practice

SOLO

Practising this on your own can be quite difficult. The best method I can suggest is to play a boast from about the service box area then try to retrieve it as a short crosscourt lob and so repeat the boast off the lob. This exercise can be very tiring and therefore can only be done for a short period.

PAIRS

1 One partner plays an attacking boast while the other returns it as a crosscourt shot. The first then returns it straight down the wall to length and the other plays an attacking boast trying to keep the

Dean Williams and Ahmed Safwat are both renowned exponents of the boast

ball low and flat with a margin for error. This routine then repeats until a mistake is made.

2 Play a straight rally to length down either the backhand or forehand side. Both players have the option to play a boast whenever they consider it appropriate, preferably when the ball is left short of a length or one partner has not recovered to the 'T'. When the boast is played the partner must try to return the ball across court to length for the rally to continue down the wall again. To make the practice more interesting you could play the rally up to fifteen points American scoring and then repeat along the opposite side wall. This routine is also good for practising straightening down the side walls.

(Opposite) Ahmed Safwat plays the ball late with the racket low

The short angle

The short angle can be played off a loose ball in the front of the court and is used to

(Below) The forehand short angle: Hunt reaches out to take the ball behind his leading foot

The reverse angle shot is played with a high backswing. The ball is taken from in front of the leading foot and hit across to the opposite side wall

deceive your opponent or catch him wrong-footed. Disguised swing and footwork make the shot effective.

You can either make the ball trickle gently around the angle from the side wall onto the front wall and drop with no pace and little bounce to the floor, or play the ball at the side wall more sharply so that it goes across the face of the front wall, touching fairly low, and finishes on the opposite side of the court.

SWING AND POSITION

The idea is to move on to the ball well balanced and early before it reaches the top of its bounce. The leading foot must be ahead of the ball and the racket face angled so as to push or hit the ball on to the side wall sharply.

The racket can be prepared with a high backswing as if to drive the ball or it can be left low and covered with the body. You can use the wrist slightly on this shot to get the racket face at the correct angle which should be slightly open, then push or hit the ball on to the side wall first. Before playing the shot make sure that there is enough room between the side wall and the ball to allow you to get a small amount of follow through, otherwise the ball will get trapped. To get the best effect from this shot, line yourself up as if to play a straight drop or drive, then, at the last second, move slightly ahead of the ball and hit the shot flat, or with a slightly opened face, on to the side wall.

Practice

SOLO

Individual practice for this shot can be very interesting because you are not only playing the shot but also working on your fitness at the same time. Start by playing either a forehand or backhand angle on to the side wall, move across the court following the ball and repeat the angle on the other hand. Try to keep this exercise going as long as you can. Count how many angles you play below the cut line without a mistake and try to improve on the number every time.

PAIRS

Play boast, angle, drive and try to keep it going between you. If you wish you could introduce a scoring system to make the practice competitive.

The reverse angle

The reverse angle, unlike the other two angle shots, must be taken in front of the body so that you can get the ball to travel away from you across the court and hit the opposite side wall first.

SWING AND POSITION

This shot should be played from a more central position than the other two so that you can get yourself around the ball properly. Move to the ball with your racket prepared with an open face. The ball can be taken on the rise, or, at the top of its bounce, or occasionally, unlike the other two shots, it may be taken late when dropping

You must be well balanced and remember to take the ball in front of your leading foot. The shot should be angled in such a way that it hits the opposite side wall, comes back across the court towards you, touches the front wall fairly low, then fades away into the front corner. Be aware that if your opponent reads the shot he will be coming towards you at the same time as the ball, therefore you will be out of position and in his way, which could cause you to lose the stroke either by a penalty point being awarded against you, or by your opponent playing the shot away from you, and out of reach.

Practice

SOLO

Position yourself in an open place between the front wall and the short line. Play reverse angles from either the forehand or backhand side, which will keep coming back across court to you so that you can repeat them.

PAIRS

Play the following routine: boast, reverse angle, drive, which will enable you both to play reverse angles on opposite sides of the court. After practising on one side, change over and practise on the other.

POINTS TO REMEMBER ABOUT ANGLE SHOTS

1 Angle shots rely on deception. Get to the ball early and try to 'show' your opponent another shot.
2 On the short angle or the attacking boast make sure that there is enough space between the ball and the side wall. Don't try to play the shot when the ball is too tight to the side wall.
3 The reverse angle comes back towards you so make sure that you are able to get back to the 'T'.
4 Don't play any of these shots too high on the front wall as this will put your opponent in an attacking position in the front of the court.

The reverse angle is played in front of the body with the swing prepared high. The ball is played across the court to the opposite wall, coming back on to the front wall and finishing low in the front of the court.

Ahmed Safwat plays a reverse angle, taking the ball in front of the body and pushing it across the court

Gawain Briars returns an attacking shot from the front of the court

Defensive shots

THE BACK CORNER BOAST

This is a very useful defensive shot and is usually a good indication of improvement. Many players find that they cannot return a ball which is played deep into either the forehand or backhand back corner. Once this return is achieved it makes a potentially winning shot from your opponent invalid and now gives you the chance to continue the rally.

The position and target for this shot are the same as for the other boasts, but the ball is now played from deep in the back corner.

The biggest problem most players have when trying to get the boast out of the back corners is that they do not get themselves into the correct position. The common mistake is to move into the back corner with the ball rather than have the confidence to let it travel into the corner while you stay out yourself.

SWING AND POSITION

Imagine a ball that has been hit to a good length coming down the side wall towards the back of the court. It is going to bounce on the floor deep in the back corner, come up off the floor, hit the back wall and then bounce back out a little. To return this ball as a boast you must be positioned well away from both the back and side walls but close enough just to take one step in towards the corner and be able to touch both walls with the head of the racket at arm's length. This position should be somewhere around the back of the service box. The time to take the ball is after it has come off the back wall but before it drops too low.

The racket must be prepared when the ball travels past you into the corner. You must then step out with your leading foot and at the same time start the swing down underneath the ball with an open faced racket, keeping the wrist cocked.

You must, at this time, be facing either the back corner or the back wall, with your knees and back bent, and you must keep your eye on the ball until the stroke has been completed.

Swing the racket through from this position, trying to lift the ball as high onto the side wall as you possibly can, making it angle forward from the body and take an upward path across the court towards the front corner to strike the front wall a safe height above the tin.

If you are in trouble and the shot needs to be really safe it can hit the front wall fairly high around the cut line; but if you feel you are in control then it is a good idea to make the shot lower and strike the front wall, side wall, floor. This will sometimes find you the nick as with the attacking boast.

Do not make the mistake of aiming the shot too far forward along the side wall as it will come back down the middle of the court. Also remember that you have played a defensive shot so make sure that as soon as you have finished the stroke you move quickly to the 'T' to be ready to

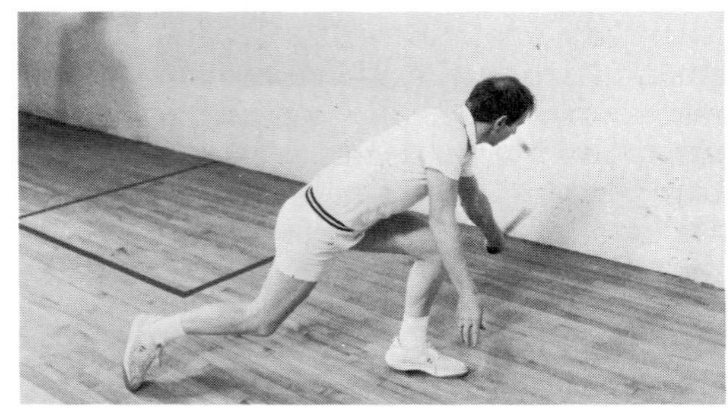

The back corner boast. Try to lift the ball as high on to the side wall as you can. It should angle forward from the body and take an upward path across the court towards the opposite corner

cover any attacking shot that your opponent might play.

Practice

SOLO
If you are just beginning to play this shot it will be best to use a white or red dot ball. Stand well out of the back corner on about the back outside edge of the service box, facing into the corner. Throw the ball fairly high to start with around the angle, back wall, side wall, floor. While throwing the ball prepare your swing, step forward by moving only one foot towards the corner, bend your knees, keep your eye on the ball, stay balanced and play the boast. If, as a result of your shot, the ball comes back across court from the opposite front corner, then you have played the shot well.

PAIRS
The best exercise is for one of you to play straight drives to length down the side walls while the other continually plays boasts and recovers to the 'T'. This way you will practise both forehand and backhand boasts plus forehand and backhand drives to length.

THE BACK WALL BOAST

The back wall boast is a shot that you should try to use as little as possible as it can easily be put away by your opponent at the front of the court. It is useful to know how to play the shot but it should really only be used as a last resort.

The aim is to hit the ball as high on the back wall as you can so that it lifts high over the court into either of the front corners. The best results are achieved by aiming the ball diagonally across the court to land in the opposite front corner as tight into the corner as possible. If played well the ball will come off the front wall parallel to the side wall, making the return difficult to play. The shot can also be aimed to go straight down the wall on the same side of the court, but you must take care as plenty of height is needed for this and it can very often result in the ball touching the side wall out of court.

The back wall boast. Aim to hit the ball as high on the back wall as you can so that it lifts over the court into either of the front corners

SWING AND POSITION

As with the boast from the back corner you must stay well out of the back of the court to give yourself a chance of getting the shot to work. On the forehand side it is best to face the back wall whereas on the backhand side you should be facing the side wall. Remember that if you are in your forehand back corner you will be playing a backhand back wall boast and vice versa.

You must prepare the swing, especially on the backhand side. Occasionally, on the forehand side, you can play the shot with a shortened backswing. When swinging you must get the racket to come underneath the ball with the face well open, which will give the ball the necessary lift up on to the back wall to make the return effective. Do not stop the racket at the point of impact, but continue the swing through the ball, otherwise, without a follow through, the ball will land short of the front wall.

If the ball you are about to play has not

The back wall boast: hit through the ball and follow through

bounced very high, to help get the necessary lift you must bend your back and knees so that you get well underneath the shot. If you should get too close to either the back wall or the ball, one of the following three disasters will occur!

1 You will stun the shot.

2 It could come off the back wall and hit you.

3 You could end up with a broken racket by following through on to the back wall.

REMEMBER: Stay away from the wall!

Practice

SOLO

Throw the ball on to the back wall, stay far enough away to be able to swing the racket through and try the shot. If the ball lands short of the front wall it does not necessarily mean that you are not hitting it hard

enough but more often that you are not getting underneath the ball and hitting it high enough. Keep practising one at a time until you can get the shot to work regularly.

PAIRS
Get your practice partner to play some length shots which are not too close to the side wall but go well into the back of the court. Let the ball go past you and then play the back wall boast one side at a time, aiming the shot to return straight down the same side of the court. After practising straight back wall boasts on both sides, change the routine by aiming your shot diagonally to practise crosscourt back wall boasts. To achieve this just turn the body a little further round towards the centre of the back wall. Your partner will play straight drives off your boasts to enable you to practise on alternate sides.

THE SKID BOAST

This is another shot, like the back wall boast, that you will not play too often. The reason for using it is usually as a form of deception rather than as a defensive boast. Its only use as a defensive shot is to force your opponent off the 'T' to the back of the court.

The target to aim for is very high in either front corner of the court. The ball must hit the side wall first as close to the out of court line as you can get it and come in towards the vertical line between side wall and front wall. It should then hit the front wall and screw across the court, out of your opponent's reach, to land in the opposite back corner as deep as possible. If played well the ball can also hit the opposite side wall before landing and kick out awkwardly into the back of the court. This shot is one of the ways of making the ball hit all four walls before the floor. It is a very good exhibition shot. Ask the top pro in your area to demonstrate it for you sometime.

SWING AND POSITION

To be successful this shot can be played from any easy ball down either side wall. Ideally it should not be really tight in either the front or back corner and should be away from the side wall. Position yourself with your body facing the side wall and have your backswing prepared. You must be well balanced, either moving on to the ball or in a steady position when the ball gets to you. The racket should be accelerated through quickly to come up underneath the ball and give it the necessary lift to get it into the top front corner, plus the power to make it all the way around and over the court. When you have made the impact do not stop the swing, follow through well. This is the reason why the ball must be well away from the side wall. Also do not try to lift the ball with your body, keep the body still and hit the ball to the target by swinging your arm rather than your body, otherwise you could pull the ball out of court.

Practice

SOLO

Feed a ball a few feet (a metre or so) away from the side wall to about the service box area. Take the ball at the top of its bounce, racket well prepared, swing underneath the ball and lift it high into the front corner, striking the side wall first as close into the corner as possible. This should result in a high ball travelling diagonally across court to the opposite back corner. It is best to try the forehand side first, get some success, then try the backhand.

POINTS TO REMEMBER ABOUT BOASTS

1 Stay well away from the back corner.
2 Open the racket face and get the ball to lift well up on to the side wall.
3 Do not try to lift the ball with movement from the shoulders or body.
4 Move quickly to the 'T' after playing the shot.

THE LOB – CROSSCOURT AND STRAIGHT

The crosscourt lob. The racket face must be very open, coming up underneath the ball to push it slowly as high as possible on to the front wall

The lob can be used from any part of the court and is a very useful defensive shot that will help to give you time when under pressure. It is also a way of exposing your opponent if he is not very good at taking defensive volleys. The best time to play a lob is when your opponent has the advantage and plays a good short shot in the front of the court. The lob can also be very useful when played from the front of the court, across court, with your opponent behind you on the 'T'.

The lob should be aimed to hit the front wall high. On the crosscourt this should be as near to the out of court line as possible, but on the straight lob perhaps a little lower. The ball will then have early lift on it, which means that it should be out of your opponent's reach when he is on the 'T' or in the centre of the court.

To progress from playing the crosscourt lob out of reach of the centre of the court, you should try to get the ball to a good width. This means that it should strike the opposite side wall high, at about the back of the service box, which makes the volley

The straight lob. The ball is taken level with or just ahead of the leading foot. Try to keep the ball

return harder for your opponent to play.

The straight lob obviously cannot have the same width applied to it but should be kept as straight as possible and just in from the side wall, so that if the shot lifts above the out of court line the ball will not touch the side wall out of court and ruin a perfectly good shot.

After hitting a good width the ball should land to a good length in the back corners of the court, preferably hitting the floor and having a slight bounce on to the back wall. This puts your opponent under pressure to volley the ball, because if he allows it to land, a return is very difficult. This applies to both crosscourt and straight lobs.

CROSSCOURT LOB, SWING AND POSITION

Approach this shot on an arc from the 'T'. On either side of the court, make sure that you take the ball well in front of the body. When playing a forehand lob it is best to open the stance out a little towards the front wall, whereas on the backhand side you should position yourself facing the side wall. It is best to stretch the last step to the ball, leaving the back foot behind as an anchorage point. This also enables you to get down low. On the forehand side you can play off either foot, but on the backhand it is best to play off the leading foot.

The racket does not need a high prepared swing but should be short because you are not trying to generate any power. The racket face should be very open, coming up underneath the ball, to push it slowly as high as possible on to the front wall.

After the racket has made contact with the ball do not stop but follow well through, otherwise the ball will not carry into the back of the court. To ensure that you get enough lift on the shot you must bend your back and knees to get well under the shot. Remember not to swing

parallel and just off the side wall as high as possible, finishing to a good length in the back corner

the racket too fast, otherwise the ball will keep going out of court, not because it has been hit too high but because it has been hit too hard.

Try to aim the ball up to half way across the front wall on your side, to ensure that the lob does not go out of court on the side walls too often. Keep adjusting your aim until you find the spot that gives you a good length.

STRAIGHT LOB, SWING AND POSITION

The method for playing the straight lob is exactly the same as for the crosscourt lob, but your position around the ball changes. Instead of taking the ball well in front of the body you must get slightly further round it and take it level with, or just ahead of, the leading foot. Once again the forehand can be played off either foot but the backhand is best played off the leading foot. Do not aim the ball quite so high on the front wall as you would for the crosscourt lob but try to keep it parallel and just off the side wall as high as possible at the short line, finishing to a good length in the back corner.

Practice

SOLO

Practising crosscourt lobs on your own is quite difficult unless you are extremely fit, in which case you can play a side wall boast, move to the front of the court, return the boast as either a crosscourt or straight lob, then re-boast the lob and see how long you can continue the rally. This, therefore, makes very good fitness training.

PAIRS

1 You can feed a boast while your partner moves from the 'T' and plays either a crosscourt or straight lob which you then boast again and the exercise repeats.

2 If you wish to progress from this you could play boast, lob (either straight or across), straight return, then both of you will play all the shots and move up and down the court during the rally.

POINTS TO REMEMBER ABOUT LOBS

1 Always reach out for the lob, stretch the last step.
2 Get well under the ball, bend at the back and knees.
3 Open the racket face and push, do not hit, from underneath the ball. You are playing a slow shot that will go out of court if hit too hard.
4 Make sure that after the point of contact of racket and ball you keep the racket following through.
5 Hit the ball as high on the front wall as possible: just above the cut line is not high enough.
6 Keep your aim on your side of the front wall up to half way across, otherwise you will get too much width and the ball will go out of court.
7 Lobs are not necessarily played from the front of the court. A good lob serve is difficult to return. A crosscourt lob from the back of the court is a good way of getting your opponent off the 'T'. The targets are the same, high on the front wall out of reach of the centre of the court, landing to a good length in the back corners.

(Below) Hiddy Jahan plays a lob at full stretch

(Right) Soheil Qaiser reaches to play a lob

Ready to go on the perspex court:
the World Masters match between Gawain Briars and Stuart Davenport

BOB LINCOLN

Part Four: Preparation for matchplay

INTRODUCTION

This section of the book will guide you through match preparation, helping you to miss the many pitfalls in training and also guarantee that you are not wasting time. It is for all levels of squash players, ranging from the beginner to the international player, and does take into account that you may have limited time for training. Divided into two sections, long term and short term, it shows how to prepare carefully for a match in the future. Before we start looking at training, let us first look at the important elements of the squash game – they are listed below. I would like you to list them in order of priority.

Fitness
Tactics
Technique
Determination to win

The solution to the test is:

1 Tactics
2 Determination
3 Technique
4 Fitness

1 **Tactics** – It is of little use to train for hours to become extremely fit and develop a good technique only to play the ball continually back to your opponent. It is important to have a good sound knowledge of tactics in order to win. They will be the deciding factor in a tight match.

2 **Determination** – If you go on court with someone of a similar standard and are not determined, all of your training will be wasted. Determination is something that should be looked at before a long training programme is undertaken.

3 **Technique** – Fitness training means that with poor technique you will only postpone defeat. It is of little use getting extremely fit to hit the ball into the tin.

4 **Fitness** – When you know where you are trying to hit the ball, you are determined and your technique is sound, then fitness becomes an important part of the game. It is not, however, its most important aspect.

Long-term preparation

HOW TO DEVISE A TRAINING PROGRAMME

1 Squash skill is the most important element in any training programme. If you have only limited time to dedicate to squash, concentrate on working on court, either alone or with a partner.

2 Ensure you are getting plenty of matchplay. Training alone is of limited value. The experience gained from matchplay cannot be replaced by solo practices.

3 Your fitness programme must be designed for squash. You need stamina to last five long games. You need speed to move around the court, and after intensive bursts of energy you need to be able to recover quickly. Muscle endurance is required to run around the court and work the racket effectively to produce strokes. You need flexibility for good reach and also of course to lessen the danger of injury. As you get fitter, the body fat reduces to lower levels, which makes you work more efficiently.

4 Ensure some fitness work takes place on court, by playing and doing fitness training that is related to squash.

5 Background fitness work should be geared to overall body development. Playing a racket sport such as squash can develop one side of the body more than the other and this can affect your overall flexibility. It could also create problems in later life. Therefore, make sure your training programme works the whole of your body systematically, using both arms and both legs. Careful planning and progression is the secret to improving fitness. Increase the amount of training gradually. Working flat out day after day will upset your metabolism, make you feel unwell and totally unfit to train or play.

6 Your training programme should be for a set period of time. You can work for three weeks, six weeks, eight weeks, but do ensure that the period has a definite final date. Continuous training becomes monotonous and is of limited value.

7 Ensure you taper down any training immediately before a competition. Otherwise you will only tire yourself, undermine your confidence and skills and be unable to play properly. This will of course bring about a depression and make you wonder why you had been bothering to train at all!

8 Squash players often lose out by not keeping an accurate training log. Most athletes would have every single element of training in writing, including diet sheets. It is important to keep an accurate training diary, so that you are aware of your exact achievements. Also note down injuries and any side effects, pain or fatigue that lasts over from any particular training session. Make sure training programmes are well balanced. Specific areas will be weak and should be concentrated on, but the programme should be well balanced overall. Rest and recovery are important. They should be built into your programme, allowing at least one or two days off per week. Training too hard can be counter productive. You must allow for recovery.

9 Most of the training should be done out of season, in the summer. Throughout the competitive season, lighter training can be maintained, although odd days of training will not improve fitness. A well planned programme will build up fitness year by year. You need not worry about losing it, as the body loses its fitness much more slowly than it gains. So, if you need time for studying or work, or to recover from illness or injury, do not concern yourself with a possible loss of fitness.

Zaman is one of the world's great natural squash talents

PLANNING FOR A BALANCED PROGRAMME

If you draw out a month planner and write in all the important fixtures or work requirements needed throughout the month, you can then allocate certain sections for training. It is advisable to spend twice as much time with the racket as in training for fitness; also the fitness elements in your programme must balance each other. If you decide on different types of training in any one session, make sure you complete any explosive speed training in the first part of the session and any anaerobic training last. Alternate high workloads with relatively easy sessions. For instance, if you do a punishing interval training session, follow it with an easy jog or a swim.

A good training programme should include the following:

1 Passive stretching, i.e. flexibility work, every day if possible. (See 'Warm-Up', page 133).
2 Court practice of varied kinds as often as possible.
3 Aerobic training for stamina two or three days a week. (see page 129).
4 Anaerobic training (local muscle endurance) two or three days a week. (see page 129).
5 Explosive speed training three times a week. (see page 130).

Jahangir Khan, the supremely fit player

SAFETY FACTORS

NEVER
1 try to play through injury, pain or do any exercise or activity which causes pain.
2 exercise after an illness, especially with a raised temperature, or with muscle soreness during or after a bout of flu.
3 train if you feel run down or over-fatigued.

If for some reason you have to stop training, for example if you go on holiday or have a heavy work commitment, re-start the programme at a lower level and gradually build up again over a few weeks.

Try to maintain a properly balanced diet, including fresh fruit, vegetables, meat, eggs, carbohydrates, cheese or fish and fibre. Resist the temptation to fill up with junk foods. Try to have three meals a day, but avoid overloading the stomach at any time. Do not play or train within two or three hours of a meal. During a hard training day, it is advisable to avoid spicy or fried foods, and avoid heavy meals.

Try to drink plenty of water every day, especially if you suffer from cramps. If necessary, there are replacement drinks on the market. If you continue to suffer from cramp problems, consult your doctor. Do not drink too much tea, coffee or fizzy drinks, but if you do, drink a glass of water afterwards.

WEAKNESSES

We have looked at the main aspects of the game briefly and also run through important points for developing and planning out a programme to train for a match. Now we must examine your specific weaknesses to determine which area of your game needs concentrating on.

ity

EVALUATION SHEET FOR SQUASH PLAYERS

How to use this sheet:

1. Use a 10 point scale to evaluate your own strong and weak points.
2. Ask the coach/team mate/friend/opponent to rate you on each item.
3. Next to each item write A, B, C, D, E: A excellent – E poor.
4. Fill in the first column for forehand and the second for backhand.
5. General comments.

Execution of basic shots

	F/H	B/H
Grip V formed by thumb and forefinger.		
Racket head up. Cocked wrist between shots.		
Transfer of weight on to front foot.		
Swing: elbow bent and close to side.		
Follow through: straight apart from crosscourt.		
Volley, smash, stop volley, short swing.		
Length: ball bounces behind service box.		
generally aims at cut line.		
varies according to bounce, strength.		
Accuracy close to wall into corners.		
Pace, variation of pace.		
Boast, high defensive to move the opponent.		
Lob, hit side wall into corners.		
Drop, accuracy, cut, disguise		
Serve.		
Return of service, mainly high along side wall.		

A squash court can sometimes seem a small place for two people. (Opposite) Bryan Beeson and Geoff Williams

Movement

Head and eyes turn to watch ball between shots.	________	________
Shoulders face side wall when hitting the ball.	________	________
Balance?	________	________
Control of T centre of court between shots.	________	________
Speed to the ball, off the mark.	________	________
Speed away from ball after hitting.	________	________
Flowing movements, long strides, not jerky.	________	________
Relaxed, not too tense but not asleep.	________	________
Anticipation, bend knees between shots, move.	________	________
Face back wall to get ball out of corners.	________	________

Court craft and tactics

Unforced errors kept to minimum, keep ball in play.	________	________
Conservation of energy, avoid needless bustling.	________	________
Moving opponent to corners, especially back corners.	________	________
Applying pressure, taking the ball early.	________	________
Defence shots – tight.	________	________
Attack from opponent's weak shots.	________	________
Hitting outright winners.	________	________
Adapting game to ball, court, opponent.	________	________
Patience.	________	________
Deception.	________	________
Temperament match play – crucial point.	________	________
Determination.	________	________
Hand in – play more attacking shots.	________	________
Hand out – get server away from T; avoid errors.	________	________
Stay in front of opponent – play deep shots.	________	________
Cut off and volley whenever possible.	________	________
Avoid setting up easy shots for opponent.	________	________
Beware of hitting balls across the court.	________	________

Study opponent's shots during the knock up and game.	______	______
Avoid opponent's strong points.	______	______
Concentrate on opponent's weaknesses.	______	______
If you are losing, try other tactics.	______	______
Unsettle opponent by varying pace and lobbing.	______	______
When in command, do not relax.	______	______
Keep opponent under pressure.	______	______
Concentrate – avoid looking at gallery and talking.	______	______

Fitness

Cardio-respiratory ('aerobic fitness').	______	______
Muscle strength.	______	______
Local muscle endurance ('anaerobic fitness').	______	______
Mobility.	______	______
Body fat content.	______	______

Comments

When you have completed the chart you will have found the areas of weakness relating to your game. Now we must set about rectifying these weaknesses.

HOW TO CORRECT WEAKNESSES IN YOUR GAME

1 Execution of basic shots

This area has been covered comprehensively in the other parts of the book. When planning a programme, however, it is important to quantify what you are doing. This can be done by logging down the results in your training book. For example, when practising lengths by striking the ball down the wall for ten minutes, set yourself a target and see how many times you can land the ball in that particular area. As you improve, make the target areas more difficult and try to beat your last best score.

Always plan out practice sessions.

2 Movement

The best way to practise movement is by 'ghosting', a technique used to groove movement patterns by careful repetition. Ghosting is playing a rally without a ball, the emphasis being placed on the quality of the movement and swing while remembering to watch the execution of your shots during the rally. Ghosting is also useful in developing anaerobic fitness (local muscle endurance).

Another method of improving movement around the court is by doing routines with a partner. By continuously repeating the same movements and shot patterns, it is possible to develop economical and efficient movements to ensure not only that you can cover the court smoothly and quickly but also that you do not waste an enormous amount of energy.

3 Court craft and tactics

One of the marvellous things about squash is that you do not have to be a gifted athlete to reach the highest level of the game. By selecting a style of play that suits your physique and ability, you can achieve success.

Listed below is a chart that shows the different types of tactical play that can be used, together with methods of playing against them.

When you start to analyse the weaknesses in your game you may feel like giving up

10
PILKINGTON

ADVANCED TACTICS

Type of play	How to employ it	How to counteract it
1 Attritional	Command of 'T' Use of volley Taking ball early Percentage game Good use of length	Slow game down Use of lob Tight side wall shots Use of drop shot Winners when appropriate
2 Attacking	Emphasis on pace Aggressive play Winners played whenever there is an opportunity	Tight length Avoid the winning strength of opponent Sometimes play deliberately to strength to exploit error Slow game down
3 Slow	Lob/Drop shot Slow side wall shot	Inject pace Use both good width and length Run for every ball
4 Defensive	Retrieving type of game with use of boast. Few winning shots	Keep attacking but avoid taking risks Be prepared for long rallies
5 Variation of pace	Change of game Use of hard game and slow game	Try to adapt to the variation in pace and impose own game on it
6 Short game	Use of subtle touch play. Tactic for cold courts. Slow opponent	Be prepared to run for everything Keep in front of 'T' Try to keep opponent behind by hitting to a tight length

Squash is a simple game! It is the players and the coaches who make it seem complicated. Intricate tactics are difficult to put into practice when under pressure. Try to do the simple things really well and let your opponent do the difficult things badly.

In all the styles of play listed above, the fundamental element is length. Its important that you understand that the whole of the game is totally dependent on its quality. Unfortunately however, length will be insufficient to win against a worthy opponent. It is therefore necessary to back up deep shots with an attacking short game. The hardest tactical problem to solve is to decide when to hit to the back and when to play to the front.

Jonah Barrington had such good control of length that the opponent was buried deep in the court with very little choice of reply. He was always therefore well balanced and in position. Qamar Zaman has great flair and natural ability and is able to hit devastating shots from anywhere on the court. He is, however, extremely quick around the court which enables him to recover from difficult positions created by his adventurous play.

A good length forces your opponent on to the defensive. The ball is thirty-two feet (ten metres) away from the front wall and it is therefore difficult to attack without making a mistake. Provided you are well balanced on the 'T' and watching the ball, it should be impossible for your opponent to play a shot that cannot be covered easily. After all, you have thirty-two feet of reaction time!

A ball at the front of the court at the wrong time provides your opponent with a large choice of shots. If he has time to disguise his intentions, it will be difficult to return his shot safely as you only have about two feet (one metre) of reaction time.

The secret of success is to strike the right combination of lengths and attacking shots. If every ball were driven to length, your game would be very predictable and your opponent would simply hang back. It is necessary to use the short game to force him to cover all of the court. After burying your opponent in the back corner and forcing a weak return, attack him while he is still out of position. This will ensure that he has to run and stretch to reach your shot and keep him under sufficient pressure to prevent him from disguising his intentions.

4 Psychology

The will to win is something you are born with. It is important before setting out on a long hard training programme to determine whether you have the inbuilt desire to win. Having decided that you are prepared to push yourself for that final result, then experience is the most important factor in helping to control your emotions as well as technical and physical skills under pressure.

Play as many hard and competitive matches as possible, preferably against people a bit better than yourself. Join a league system to ensure plenty of variety of opponents and once you are good enough play for the club side and enter tournaments.

Avoiding a challenge shows mental weakness. It is common amongst players who feel they are of a good standard to avoid playing certain matches for fear of losing. Once you are frightened of losing, all sorts of mental problems occur. Take each new challenge as it comes and think only of winning.

5 Fitness – The best way to train for squash is to play

Training must be relevant to sport. Squash requires cardio-vascular endurance (aerobic stamina), local muscle endurance (anaerobic), strength, speed and mobility.

A AEROBIC FITNESS Cardio-vascular endurance.
Endurance is limited by the ability of the heart to supply oxygen to the working muscles throughout a tough match.

Efficient training can produce a 30 per cent improvement in this area.

Testing – Harvard Step Test
This system has been used for testing National Squad players for over five years.

The player steps at a rate of 30 steps per minute (a metronome is essential for accuracy) on to a bench 18″/45 cm (women) or 20″/50 cm (men) high for a period of 5 minutes.

After one minute's rest the pulse is taken for ½ minute and the fitness index calculated with this formula:

$$\text{Fitness index} = \frac{\text{Time in seconds} \times 100}{\text{Pulse for } \tfrac{1}{2}\text{ mn} \times 5.5}$$

On this index

95–105	Club player
100–110	County player
105–125	International player
125 +	World class

If you do not reach the required level, you will need to follow a special programme to increase your cardio-vascular endurance.

Training for stamina
1 Running – Start with no more than 5 minutes of steady running. Remember to build up gradually, week by week, to about thirty minutes. Use about 80–90 per cent effort which is quite a hard pace, aiming at 6–7 minute miles. In your 30 minutes you should cover 4–5 miles (6–8 kilometres).

It was Jonah Barrington who first made many squash players aware of the vital importance of fitness

Important points to remember: (i) Vary running surfaces. Road/grass/running track. Avoid slippery, loose or uneven surfaces. Change routes regularly. (ii) You must use the correct running shoes with well cushioned soles. (iii) Do not run every day!
2 Skipping – Start with 5 minutes of skipping, using alternate feet. Keep up an even, medium speed. Aim to do 1,000 skips per 7½ minutes. Build up to 30 minutes of skipping.
Important point: Wear trainers to skip. If you cannot use a squash court, skip on carpet.

B LOCAL MUSCLE ENDURANCE
Local muscle endurance in the legs and in the playing arm is needed to be able to play long rallies without fatigue.

Testing: It is difficult to test local muscle endurance. However, a good indication can be given by squat thrusts for the legs and weight lifts for the arms.

Squat thrusts	15 poor	35 average	65 excellent
Press ups	5 poor	20 average	50 excellent
Chins	2 poor	8 average	15 excellent

Training: Ghosting on court, working at high intensity, is the best form of training local muscle endurance.

Programme
Start with 6 intervals of 30 seconds of work, followed by 30 seconds of rest. Build up in each session by one extra interval of work, allowing the same rest phase, until you are doing 12 work/rest bursts.

Then do 6 intervals of work for 35 seconds, with 35 seconds rest intervals building up again to 12.

Repeat with 40 seconds intervals.

N.B. Do all other types of training before the anaerobic session, although it is a good idea to sometimes do solo ball practice afterwards to help you concentrate when tired.

C STRENGTH

Leg strength in particular is important in squash to provide a fast push off and arm strength to hit the ball hard. Stronger muscles also help to prevent injury.

Testing arm strength Using a grip dynamometer, the best of 3 tries is recorded.

	Men	Women
Minimum	50 kg	40 kg

Training: Weight circuits can be devised to build up strength but this must be carefully selected for the individual and monitored by an expert.

D SPEED

There is a need in squash to be able to move very quickly over a short distance, stop, turn and push off again.

Testing: 50 m run: run from a start line and touch a 50 m marker and walk back again. Best of three attempts.

Training: because of the build up of oxygen debt after 10–15 seconds at maximum speed, the work intervals must be kept to this length with a rest period of 45–50 seconds, so that each run can beat maximum speed.

Corner runs are done by starting from the 'T' and running to touch with a foot a mark on the floor a racket's length from the corner. Return to the 'T', then run to the next corner. Work flat out for 10–15 seconds touching as many corners as possible. Rest 45–50 seconds and repeat. Gradually build up in each session to 20 repetitions.

Short-term preparation

PRE-MATCH

1 Taper down your training at least seven days in advance.
2 Enjoy a good evening meal which includes plenty of carbohydrates.
3 Get to bed quite early.
4 Do not 'dry out' for a match, but throughout the day drink plenty of water or a diluted 'isotonic' drink.
5 Unless you have found it necessary through experimentation, do not eat within three hours of the match.
6 If at all possible have an easy day – some professionals like to hit up for an hour in the morning.
7 Pack your kit carefully (including a pair of soft soled shoes for slippery floors). It is most distressing to arrive and discover you have forgotten your shorts – and it was not supposed to be an exhibition match!

At the club

1 Arrive early, especially if you are driving at night, your eyes and body will need time to adjust.
2 If you are unfamiliar with the club check out the courts, looking for:
(a) Floor – sealed, and therefore could be slippery.
(b) Ceiling – is it low or high (could you lob your way out of trouble?).
(c) Tin – any posters that may be distracting.
(d) Temperature – if it is cold, short rallies, accurate drops and lengths difficult to return. If it is hot, long rallies; fitness will be important, as well as patience. It will be difficult to hit winners.

3 Get changed quite early to allow plenty of time for your warm up.

Gamesmanship – the art of winning games without actually cheating! Gamesmanship is an element in sport which cannot be totally ignored. An experienced opponent will split his ploys into three sections:
1 The pre-game: the intention here is to try to talk you out of the game or break your confidence and concentration. Such ploys include (i) turning up late (ii) pretend to have forgotten something (iii) dress strangely (iv) claim to have an injury or conversely tell you about his great fitness and his wins because of it.
2 The game itself: now the game has started, ploys to put you off or make you feel cheated include (i) delaying tactics between points (ii) joking with the audience and marker (iii) telling you how lucky he is being today.
3 Afterwards: after the game, if you have won, the gamesman will carefully undermine your confidence so that you do not enjoy your victory.

If you would like to know more about

gamesmanship, read the amusing book *The Complete One-Upmanship* by Stephen Potter.

Gamesmanship does not turn you into a better squash player, so remember your training and talk back with your racket.

Mental preparation

Mental preparation for a squash match is vital if you wish to perform well. It is not a factor that can be left to chance.

1 Relaxation – The first stage in mental preparation is to relax. The level required varies from person to person and on the occasion. Complete relaxation increases speed of reaction, restores balance and gives awareness. It helps to clear the mind of day to day events and reduces tension.

How to relax:

Sit still with your hands resting face down on your legs.

Close your eyes.

Allow each limb in turn to go heavy, feeling the weight increase downwards with each exalation of breath.

Practice will be required to develop the right technique and also will aid you in discovering how much time you personally need to spend on it.

2 Arousal – After relaxation, it will be necessary to wind yourself up for the match. The amount of 'psyching up' depends on your character.

Introverts tend to get easily excited and will not require a great deal of building up;

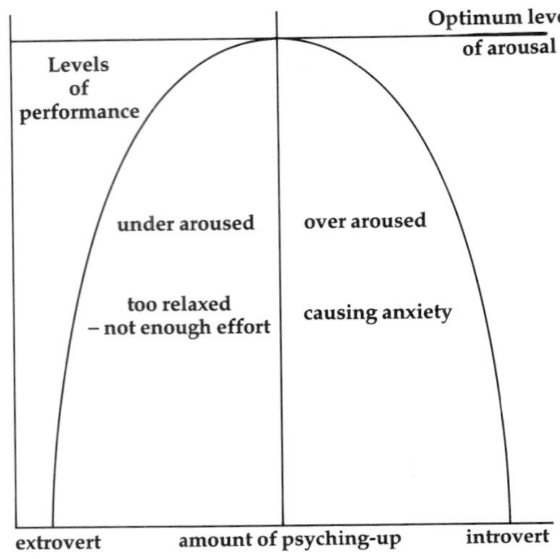

Are you sufficiently aroused?

if anything, they have to remain calm and not let nervousness take over. Extroverts, however, tend to have too much confidence which might lead to casualness and need plenty of building up in order to perform well.

Practice is the only way of learning how to reach your optimum level of arousal. If under-aroused you will not try hard enough; be over-aroused and you will suffer from anxiety and make mistakes.

Use your log book to read through and remind yourself of all the hard work you have done, this will give you confidence.

While warming up think through your match plan and specific tactics for this game, if you have seen your opponent play before. This will give you **purpose**.

THE WARM-UP

1 The warm-up should last at least five but preferably fifteen minutes.
2 It should consist of four parts: stretching exercises for the muscles, which should be performed statically, holding positions to feel a passive 'pull' along the tissues being stretched; mobilising exercises, which should be rapid free movements, to loosen the joints; and fast-moving exercises ('pulse-warmers') to increase cardio-respiratory functioning. The 'pulse-warmers' are less important if you are to do a steady-state session, but they must be done before a session of speed or interval training. The final part is skill 'practice'.

3 At the end of your exercise sessions, you should repeat this routine as your warm-down, concentrating especially on stretching.

Stretching exercises: (positions held still, each to be done at least three times).
1 Calves. Lean forward to rest your hands against a wall, with legs straight at hips and knees, heels flat on the ground. Hold to six seconds.
2 Quadriceps. Balance on one leg, bend the other up behind you, keeping your hips well forward. Holding your ankle, pull your heel towards your seat. Hold.

Quadriceps stretch

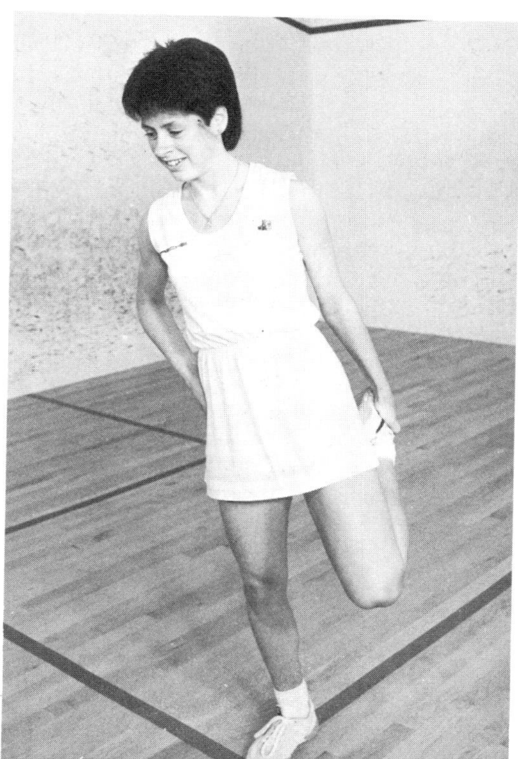

Hamstring stretch

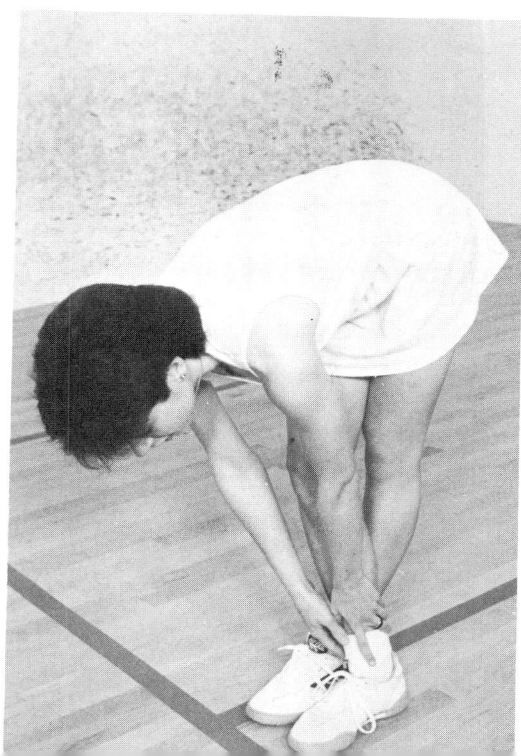

Adductor stretch

3 Hamstrings. Resting one leg forward on a support, reach forward towards your toes, bending from the hips, keeping your head up. Hold.
Or: sitting with legs straight, bend forwards from your hips. Hold.
Or: as Adductor stretch (4), but turn your toes upwards and lean over the outstretched leg, bending from the hips.
4 Adductors. Stretch one leg out sideways. Bend the other knee, to the crouch position, if possible, feeling the pull on the inside thigh of the straight leg. Hold.

Hip flexor stretch

5 Hip flexors. Stretch one leg out backwards. Bend forward knee to the crouch position. Keep back arched and hold.

Mobilising exercises: (done freely, as many times as you like).
1 Arm circling and swinging: free large circular swings with both arms, together or each in turn, alternating with high swings forwards and backwards.
2 Knee bends: slow descent, fast push-up, keeping back straight.
3 Trunk side-bending: with feet apart, bend from side to side, swinging your outside arm over your head as you bend.
4 Trunk turning: with arms held out sideways, swing from side to side, letting your outside elbow bend as you turn.
5 Hip circling: standing with feet apart, circle your hips, swinging your weight over each leg in turn.

'Pulse-warmers': exercises should be repeated at least 5 times, preferably 10. These may consist of any exercise performed as quickly as possible for ½ to 1 minute, followed by ¼ to ½ minute rest. Work/rest loads are chosen according to

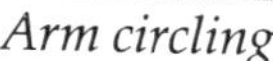

Arm circling

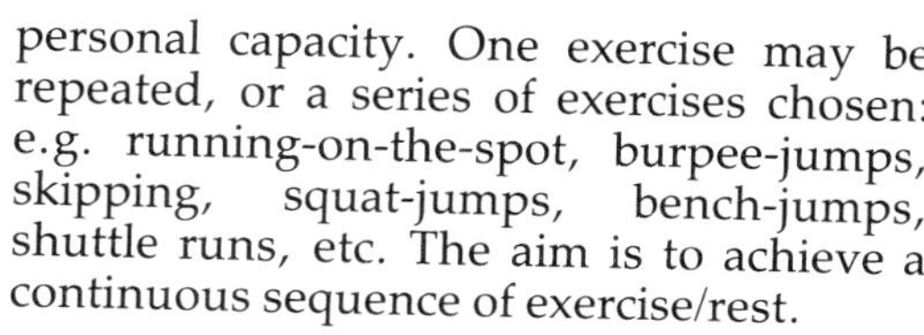

personal capacity. One exercise may be repeated, or a series of exercises chosen: e.g. running-on-the-spot, burpee-jumps, skipping, squat-jumps, bench-jumps, shuttle runs, etc. The aim is to achieve a continuous sequence of exercise/rest.

Skill 'practice': this is for concentration as well as free movement. With your racket, practise shadow strokes for a minute or two, making sure you do a perfect movement for each 'shot'. This is very important before you go on court on a cold day. It is an important moment for rehearsing your play, and planning tactics, before a tight match.

PASSIVE STRETCHING EXERCISES: FLEXIBILITY TRAINING

* Stretching muscles around a joint increases the joint's flexibility.

* To stretch a muscle, you have to hold it in its longest, fully stretched position for a count of ten.

* Passive stretching exercises are self-limiting, and therefore cannot damage the muscles.

* Don't do rapid, bouncing movements, because they tend to provoke muscular contraction, achieving the opposite of the stretching effect. If you force stretching movements beyond the muscles' natural limits, you risk tearing the muscle fibres. Hold the muscles completely still when you stretch.

* Do the stretching exercises every morning and evening, if possible. Always do some stretching exercises as part of your warm-up and warm-down routines.

* For a strained muscle, you should stretch that muscle gently 10 times, at least three or four times daily, stretching only as far as you can without feeling any pain.

* After you have recovered from a muscle injury, you must maintain the muscle's flexibility by frequent stretching. Always stretch that muscle first, before you do any other part of your warm-up or exercise session.

Robert Forde making good use of the furniture to stretch his hamstrings

Glen Brumby does a hamstring stretch in his post match warm down

MATCH PLAN

The general match plan is to use the basic game.

The basic game

Squash rallies are not won easily. You have to work your opponent out of position by moving him continually around the court before attempting to play a winner. A sound knowledge of the 'basic game' will help you achieve better results and is therefore an important weapon in your strategic armoury.

The list below will give you some indication of what the basic game is about:

1 **Attack with good length** A good length is a ball hit on to the front wall aimed carefully to make it bounce at the back of the court on the floor behind the service box; the ball must reach the back wall. The ball is still a good length if it comes off the back wall after one bounce, as this shot also takes the opponent into the back of the court. The ball should be close to the side wall. The purpose of a good length is to force the opponent away from the 'T' and into a defensive position.

2 **Control the 'T'** Every squash player must understand from the start that he can only control the game from the 'T'. You must not therefore hit the ball down the middle of the court as you will then have to vacate the 'T' position to allow your opponent to play his shot. Squash is such a fast game that any slacking spells trouble. Never leave an opening for your opponent: you must regain the 'T' before he reaches the ball.

3 **Watch the ball** Unless you watch the ball at all times, you will play like a beginner. If you find this difficult, make watching the ball a deliberate practice. Keep your head still while striking the ball and do not lift your head too early to see where your shot has gone. Watch the ball onto your racket and you will be more likely to hit from the middle of the strings.

Watch your opponent play his shot especially when he is behind you, otherwise you will be caught flat-footed. Also, as you turn to watch the ball, you lessen the risk of being hit.

4 **Vary the service** The main basic serve is a semi-lob hitting the side wall next to your opponent, but it pays to use a variation from time to time. A sudden change can often bring unexpected rewards.

5 **Return the service straight down the side wall** After his serve, your opponent has easy access to the 'T'. The basic return down the side wall takes him off the 'T' and gives you a chance to get into the rally on an even footing.

6 **Crosscourt shots must pass your opponent** If your crosscourt shots are not of a good width or length, your opponent will cut the ball off early without leaving the 'T'. This will mean that you are left stranded in one corner with the ball in another. Take great care that your crosscourts pass your opponent, forcing him back and allowing you to regain the centre position.

7 **Make your opponent run** This may seem an obvious statement. Evidently, it is futile to hit the ball consistently back to your opponent. Force him to the back with a good length, send him to the front with accurate angles and drop shots. Whenever

he is out of position, oblige him to run. The secret is to keep him guessing and keep him running. Be sure however that you can reach the 'T' before playing short shots.

8 Vary the pace By varying the pace, you make it much more difficult for your opponent to read your game or settle down in any kind of rhythm. Slow the game down when in trouble to buy time to recover to the 'T'. Speed the game up when you are in a good well-balanced position to take time away from your opponent. Mix hard hitting and floated shots to make the ball bounce at different heights.

9 Try not to be forced to boast When everything tells you to boast, don't. Your opponent will be waiting eagerly to attack your loose shot at the front of the court. If at all possible straighten the ball down the side wall with a lob to a length.

10 Volley whenever possible When you volley the ball your opponent is placed under enormous pressure. Carefully select the balls which ought to be volleyed to ensure that you are well balanced and can recover easily. Volleys are not necessarily winners but they shorten your opponent's time to reach the 'T' and therefore make it difficult for him to be well balanced for his next shot.

Specific plan

The specific match plan is applicable when you have already seen your opponent play and know his strengths and weaknesses – *see* Advanced Tactics (page 126).

The knock-up

When you open the court door and step through you should be mentally and physically prepared for the battle ahead. The knock-up is not only to warm the ball but to discover some vital information:

1 Is the court as you had assessed it earlier?

2 What is the bounce of the ball like?

3 Does your opponent have any obvious weaknesses – although these may disappear as he gets used to the ball and relaxes?

Use the knock-up thoroughly yourself:

1 Start the knock-up by hitting medium paced balls to length with a good width, being careful to hit through the ball to build up your timing and rhythm. Stand fairly deep in the court so as to have more time to position yourself correctly for each shot.

2 As you gain confidence, move forward to the short line. During the game you will want to dominate the 'T' area and therefore react from this distance to the front wall.

3 Feed your opponent a variety of shots, i.e. lobs, boasts and volleys to find out how he copes with them. The information gained might prove useful when the match begins.

4 Move around the court during the knock-up. Do not stand in one spot only, but ensure that you have played shots from all four corners.

5 If you have played your opponent before, try out all of the shots as he will have seen them before.

If on the other hand this is a new

opponent, it might be a good idea simply to play drives, concentrating on not making errors. When the match starts your opponent will not know what to expect.

Problems in the match

A five point check list will help you to solve any problems during the match:

1 Length – Is it good enough? Look and see where your drives are landing. If the quality is not good enough, change it until it is by either hitting harder/softer, or higher/lower/tighter to the wall.

2 'T' – Are you returning quickly enough to the 'T' position?

3 Eyes on the ball – Are you watching the ball wherever it goes, including behind?

4 Errors – Are you giving the game away by making too many unforced errors? Aim higher up the wall to prevent this.

5 Movement of opponent – Is your play too negative, simply hitting back to your opponent, do you need to attack more?

If after checking through and finding you do have some or all of the above problems, change your style of play accordingly.

Always change a losing game.

Squash in the round. The British Open at Wembley Conference Centre

SUMMARY

Careful preparation will help you achieve a much greater level of success. As we have seen, it should encompass several aspects. There are ways to improve your technique, increase your stamina, adjust your mental approach to a match. You can perfect all these by training consistently and above all, by playing. Regular matches against opponents of a similar or higher standard than yourself mean that you will acquire the experience which is indispensable and can bring you victory, even when playing a younger or seemingly fitter player than yourself. Squash is a wonderful sport and needs to be approached in the right spirit – it is a game and you should go out on court first and foremost to enjoy yourself.

ADDRESSES

Squash Rackets Association,
Francis House,
Francis Street,
London SW1P 1DE
Tel: 01 828 3064/6

Women's Squash Rackets Association,
345, Upper Richmond Road West,
London SW14 8QN
Tel: 01 876 6219

Scottish Squash Rackets Association,
18 Ainslie Place,
Edinburgh EH3 6AU
Tel: 031 225 2502

Welsh Squash Rackets Federation,
Trienna,
Quarella,
Bridgend,
Mid Glamorgan,
Wales
Tel: 0656 56752

Irish Squash Rackets Federation,
38, Woodlawn Park Grove,
Firhouse,
Co. Dublin
Tel: 0001 521689

The International Squash Rackets Federation,
Executive Office,
National Sports Centre,
Sophia Gardens,
Cardiff,
Wales CF1 9SW
Tel: 0222 374771

Australian Squash Rackets Association,
PO Box 356,
Spring Hill,
Queensland,
Australia 4000
Tel: (07) 221–3909

Canadian Squash Racquets Association,
333 River Road,
Ottawa,
Ontario,
Canada K1L 8H9
Tel: (613) 741–6786

The Egyptian Squash Rackets Association,
c/o Heliopolis Sporting Club,
Heliopolis,
Cairo,
Egypt

The Squash Rackets Federation of India,
c/o The Calcutta Rackets Club,
nr St Paul's Cathedral,
Chowringhee,
Calcutta,
700 071 India
Tel: 44 1152

New Zealand Squash Rackets Association,
PO Box 1040,
Tauranga,
New Zealand
Tel: Tauranga 88496

United States Squash Rackets Assoc. Inc.,
211 Ford Road,
Bala-Cynwyd,
PA 19004,
USA
Tel: (215) 667–4006